DEAF BY GIANTS
When Your Flesh is Louder than His Voice

Kara Lock-Harris

Edited by
Dominique Lambright

DEAF BY GIANTS:
When Your Flesh is Louder than His Voice

Copyright © 2018 Kara Lock-Harris

All rights reserved. No part of this book may be reproduced or transmitted in any form or by any means, electronic or mechanical, including photocopying, recording, or by any information storage and retrieval system without the written permission of the author or publisher, except where permitted by law.

ISBN: 978-1-949176-06-3 (paperback)
ISBN: 978-1-949176-15-5 (e-book)

Library of Congress Control Number: 2018909038

Edited by: DML Editing and Writing
Exterior cover design by: Newleaf Design

Published by: KRL Publishing

More about the author: www.lettersfromchrist.net

DEDICATION

IN REVERENCE
EL SHADDAI, THE ALMIGHTY GOD

I acknowledge you as the Almighty God. You allowed me to survive many trials so that I could tell someone else how you brought me through. My life is for your glory. I will shout it on mountain tops and valley lows the great things you have done. My Lord and My Redeemer. In the name of Jesus Christ! Amen!

IN MEMORIAL
MS. SUSIE MAE LOCK

Mama, who knew all of those nights of reading Little House on the Prairie books, Robert Frost, and Edgar Allen Poe would manifest in us the way it did. I always loved hearing you speak and reciting your poetry. Thank you for instilling this incredible gift in me. You are forever with me.

IN HONOR
MR. DEWAYNE HARRIS SR.

I'm so grateful to have such an incredibly supportive husband to share my life with. You were there for me at critical chapters in my life and I will always cherish our bond. Thank you for being My Covering..

To my loving family, church family, friends that I have met, and those I'll never meet. Whether you read this book or not, I had you in mind and I dedicate this book to you. Thank you for being a part of my journey. ~ Kara

TABLE OF CONTENTS

FOREWORD i

PROLOGUE iv

CHAPTER 1: SOMETHING TOLD ME 1

CHAPTER 2: DEAF BY "NEEDS" 13

CHAPTER 3: DEAF BY DRY PLACES 30

CHAPTER 4: DEAF BY BAD LOVE 44

CHAPTER 5: DEAF BY REJECTION 61

CHAPTER 6: DEAF BY ABUSING GRACE 69

CHAPTER 7: DEAF BY DEATH 82

CHAPTER 8: DEAF BY UNGUARDED HEART 99

CHAPTER 9: HE THAT HAS AN EAR 112

EPILOGUE 119

NOTES 121

ACKNOWLEDGMENTS 122

FOREWORD

So often, we are consumed by factoids, blogs, postings, or as Kara Lock-Harris notes in her book, **Deaf by Giants**, "voices" and "giants." This book is a must read because rather than telling the reader how to view the world, the book offers reasons, rationale, and reflections to guide each of us on a journey of spiritual exploration; to refocus what is important; and to remember why the voice of God is pertinent. I have known the author a little over 34 years, and in those years, I have witnessed firsthand and have been an active participant in the experiences she writes about in her book. She provides a vivid, detailed account when she writes about her personal, life-changing memories that have resulted in many shed tears and bursts of laughter. The memories and experiences equip her to be able to write this book; but, more importantly those experiences allow her to attest firsthand to the power of Jesus Christ when one submits to His voice. Upon reading the prologue alone, I was immediately reminded of the scripture that reads, *"But grow in the grace and knowledge of our Lord and Savior Jesus Christ." (2 Peter 3:18)* Kara's testimony and openness in the book demonstrate her growth and knowledge of the Lord and Savior Jesus Christ.

Kara's truth and vulnerability in the book helps her readers reflect on what is truly valuable, and through her life story, the reader will experience a path of self-discovery, self-discernment, and self-reflection. The book unfolds an amazing voyage of self-discovery, a process that I, and anyone who reads the book, can emulate. The book is a refreshing deep-dive into the most important thoughts of life, with a balanced mixture of spiritual conviction and growth. Her book is humbling, yet prompts personal accountability. Among other revelations, the book holds an obvious, yet complex, fundamental journey. A journey that infuses faith, health, agape love, varying aspects of relationship (family, romantic, work, and church); and, how through listening to God's voice, those relationships can be enhanced, renewed, or ended. I have no doubt that readers will not just take away Kara's personal experiences, but a soul-searching connection will be evoked in the reader that warrants the pondering of one's own personal experience with hearing the voice of God when the flesh becomes louder than God's voice.

My personal connections to Kara as a best friend and Sister in Christ, my professional background as an expert in the field of literacy and educational leadership, and my spiritual journey as a believer in Jesus Christ enables me to gauge her metamorphosis from personal, professional, and spiritual lenses, and provide commentary as a Foreword to her book. It is through these varying lenses that Kara is able to lift the spirits and challenge the mindsets of all who will read the book. Scripture reminds us that, "The mind governed by the flesh is death, but the mind governed by the Spirit is life and peace," Romans 8:6. It is in Kara's book that the reader will witness her submission to God's voice; hence, resulting in her having a renewed mind and living in peace. The book personifies the embodiment of Philippians 4:13, *"I can do all things through Christ, who strengthens me."* Through her obedience in listening to the voice of God; hence, conquering those giants that made many attempts to "deafen" her, Kara demonstrates in the book how she has been able to overcome life's challenges and attain varying levels of success in the personal, professional, and spiritual realms of her life. More importantly, her book captures the essence of spiritual obedience and personal development by offering an analytical and spiritual look into a multi-faceted approach of her mind, her heart, and her soul.

In service,
Dr. Vanessa R. Liederbach, Ph.D.

PROLOGUE

I used to be a part of that wicked generation Jesus often warned about, you know, those who are always needing a sign to believe. A doubting Thomas who wanted so badly to believe that there was more to life than what I was encountering every day, but I needed to touch it to believe. I knew there was a God, but my knowledge of Him was based on what others told me and not what I knew and understood for myself. With so many different ideas being shoved at me from my mother, other family members, friends, schools, society and church; it was difficult to choose a path or even know what I believed.

The voices of so many, yelling and pulling at me throughout my life caused me to be a walking collection of every person and entity I had connected with. As long as the voices around me were cheering me on and steering me the way they thought I should go, I considered life to be good. Somehow, through all the commotion, there were times I could hear something within myself that seemed to cause a searching of my deepest thoughts and desires; I normally felt this examining when I was all alone.

One evening, the feeling came along with an intense sadness in the pit of my stomach, I couldn't make sense of it. I tried to make myself feel better by going thru a checklist of everything good I had going for myself, this usually made the sad feeling go away.

Do I have a roof over my head? Check! Are my kids healthy? Check! Do I have a job? Check! Is my family doing fine? Check! But, this night the checklist didn't work. This night, I had a strong urge to talk to someone and not just anyone – God. Not a one-way prayer, but, communication. I needed Him to talk back to me. Not sure how to do this, I picked up my Bible, asked God to speak to me thru His word, and then I opened the Bible. I decided to read the beginning of whatever chapter I opened up to. Nehemiah 2 was the chapter displayed and began reading.

> *And it came to pass in the month Nisan, in the twentieth year of Artaxerxes the king, that wine was before him: and I took up the wine, and gave it unto the king. Now I had not been beforetime sad in his presence.*
>
> *2 Wherefore the king said unto me, Why is thy countenance sad, seeing thou art not sick? this is nothing else but sorrow of heart. Then I was very sore afraid,*

Quickly, I slammed the Bible closed and jumped to my feet. The hairs on my arms stood up. I could feel my ears pulling back, while goosebumps covered my body. I could feel something in the room with me. My body was gripped with fear, like Nehemiah, and my heart was beating in my ears. I took some deep breaths, sat down, and opened my Bible again. I re-read Nehemiah 2:1-2. Did God just communicate with me about the sad feeling in the pit of my stomach that I couldn't shake off with my religious checklist?

Like Nehemiah, I too was sore afraid at that very moment. I was frightened, euphoric, and almost dizzy at the thought that God actually knew or even cared that I was feeling a sadness. I figured I had better read the scripture over again slowly and try to understand what message I was supposed to receive; especially, since the creator took the time to speak directly to me in my living room. I realized God was telling me I had sorrow of heart. I did. I could finally admit it! "God, I am not happy with my life and where it seems to be headed". There, I said it! I had never dared to do this with anyone else, because I always had my shield up. Something was missing and now I understand what – God.

I was so busy with life that my spiritual life was starving. That sad, tugging feeling I was experiencing was a malnourished spirit within me trying desperately to get my attention. I was going to church, but that was it; I was just going to satisfy the need to say I attended. Since God cared enough to speak to me, He has the answer to what I need. This is the voice I needed to hear. The voice that understood me. The voice that would be honest with me and not tell me what I wanted to hear. I need more of this voice.

My skepticism was gone in that instant. I realized what I had been saying to God was not as important as what He was saying to me. No more doubting or searching for signs, all I had to do was shut out the noise in my life and listen. I now have a new checklist; one that helps me to isolate the deafening distractions that are plugging my spiritual ears. The urge to write it down in a book was pressing; I knew that urgency wasn't from me. This book has been in the works for most of my life and I couldn't hear it until now. I'd like to share with you how the Holy Spirit assisted me in isolating and conquering the manifold trials, temptations, distractions, and diversions to finally be able to hear my Lord and Savior's voice over the deafening giants.

DEAF BY GIANTS
When Your Flesh is Louder than His Voice

CHAPTER ONE

<u>SOMETHING TOLD ME</u>

Isaiah 30:21 And thine ears shall hear a word behind thee, saying, This is the way, walk ye in it, when ye turn to the right hand, and when ye turn to the left.

I made it! It was Friday and I had completed 10 days of eating only fruit and vegetables. Today, I was going to celebrate my 10-day meatless scuffle with a victory meal; whatever I desired. As various meat options danced thru my head, I couldn't make a decision on what to splurge on. I briskly walked to the mailbox, with all of the energy I had from eating healthy for 10 days, and there it was: a coupon with a picture of the juiciest bacon cheeseburger dripping with onion strings on a pretzel bun. Buy one, get one free! I could hardly believe it, this was it, my reward. I mean, the picture looked so real, it's as if I could taste the burger just holding the coupon.

I sent my husband, Wayne, a text, "We're going out for dinner tonight". My stomach was still in knots from only eating fruits and vegetables for 10 days, a reminder of how difficult of a task that was for me. I kept glancing at the coupon and smiling, it's all I could think about. As I was glaring at the picture of my prize meal, out of nowhere, a voice rang in my head, "Don't eat the burger". What? Don't eat the burger? Why not? I mean, it's been 10 days since I've eaten a decent meal, or at least what I considered decent, something with meat. My stomach was growling more by this time and I quickly dismissed that voice. I looked at the coupon again. I couldn't help but wonder how much money was spent on this good-looking coupon; this burger had to be the real deal.

I began to imagine how good the burger was going to taste, my mouth watered. Wayne couldn't get home fast enough. The kids and I were all set to go. I rushed Wayne to get cleaned up so we could head out ASAP. I was in such a great mood. The drive to the restaurant was the best, no one could say anything to wreck my frame of mind; I had a burger in view. I rushed my family into the restaurant, presented my coupon to the server with a smile and didn't even mind the extra wait. When the server brought the burgers out to our table, they were captivating and looked even better than the coupon. (How often does that actually happen?) I knew this burger was meant just for me, after all, I deserved it. Not only did the burger look attractive, but it also tasted even better than I had imagined. I was enjoying every mouthwatering, tantalizing bite. I looked around at my family and everyone was enjoying their 2 for 1 burgers.

Suddenly, I noticed that I had been chomping on this particular bite for a while and it was really chewy. I spat the glob of chewed burger into a napkin to examine it and noticed that I was not only eating the burger and fixings, but also the wax paper that divides the frozen raw beef patties while they are still in the box. In an instant, I recalled the voice, "Don't eat the burger" and it hit me like a ton of bricks. I became almost disoriented, I looked at my husband and said, "Something told me not to eat this burger". The server was apologetic and of course didn't charge us for the burger, but I left beyond dissatisfied. I began to feel nauseous wondering just how much of the wax paper I had eaten. On the dreadful ride home, I tried to process what had just happened. I began to recall how I had been struggling with losing weight. I had prayed and asked the Lord to help me lose weight because I was struggling to do it on my own. 1 Peter 5:7 NLT says, *"Give all your worries and cares to God, for He cares about you."*

I was worried about my health because I knew about my family history of high blood pressure and diabetes, so I gave it to the Lord just as His word tells us to do. Out of nowhere, my Pastor asked that we eat only fruit and vegetables for 10 consecutive days in that month. Until now, I hadn't realized that this 10-day eating plan was the Lord assisting me in my prayer for help. I jumped on the 10 day fast right away out of obedience, and I lost 15 pounds. All of this played through my mind on the gloomy ride home from the restaurant. I felt sad in the pit of my stomach and I knew it wasn't because it was digesting wax paper – I ignored the small still voice that warned me to not eat the burger that day.

Once home, I laid on the couch curled up in a fetal position, and I began to talk to the Lord. I asked Him, "Was that you telling me to not eat the burger? Why didn't I listen?" As clear as day, that same voice answered, "Because your flesh was louder than my voice". I was startled at the response that fired back at me so rapidly. I replayed the day in my mind and realized how fixated I was on the tempting coupon, so much so, that I disregarded that voice. My Spirit began groaning within me and I told the Lord I was sorry. While still curled up on the couch, I felt His arms around me, comforting me. I had made a mistake, I had failed, but He was letting me know everything will be alright.

"I want to hear you Lord, I want to have confidence in your voice when it speaks me." I laid there for what seemed like hours, in His presence, reading His word, talking to Him. At that moment, all that mattered, was He was with me; I felt His forgiveness, I felt His loving embrace all around me.

You may wonder, why would the Lord speak to me about a burger? Does the Lord even care about what we eat? Of course He does! Remember, He told

Adam and Eve what trees to eat from and what tree to not eat from. God also used a vision with food when He wanted the Apostle Peter to do something unheard of, share the gospel with gentiles. But God showed Peter in a vision of a sheet dropping down from heaven, with different animals, both kosher and non-kosher, and told Peter to "Rise, Kill and Eat." *(Acts 10:9-13)* It's not my intention to belittle how the Lord interacts with us; but to stress just how much He really desires to be a part of every aspect of our lives. Do I believe the wax paper was divinely cooked with the burger purposely? Possibly. But I do believe the experience got my attention and forced me to see how my flesh was causing me to go against the help I had specifically asked for. All things work together for good to them that love the Lord, yes, even a botched burger.

If my experience had been great at the restaurant that day, I might have never begun to search myself for what's causing me to not hear this "Something", this still small voice. My failure to hear caused the Spirit to groan within me. I allowed my physical hunger pangs and what looked good to my eye, to be louder than that voice I heard. How many other times had I gone deaf to this voice? I've gone thru failed marriages, broken friendships, money woes, and a ton of other bad decisions. Has this voice been speaking to me all along and I just couldn't hear because my flesh was screaming? How can I hear you Lord over all the noise going on around me? I knew I couldn't afford to not hear this guiding voice another time, not a single time.

Has "Something" ever told you to walk away from a relationship, a job, or even a place like a mall or a restaurant? Maybe you were invited to a party or gathering and "Something" told you not to go. Have you ever been driving and "Something" told you to go a different route? Has "Something" ever told you to be a blessing to a person by giving money or food? Admit it! Countless times I've heard people say "Something" told me to do this. I've said it myself numerous times throughout my life. What exactly is this "Something" that we give so much credit to, yet find it so easy to push aside?

One thing we know for certain about this "Something" is that it's different from the normal inner thoughts that we all have? When you hear it, you know it's unique, and so you call it "Something" because you just can't pinpoint where it came from. This "Something" doesn't speak to us all the time, but always at the right time. It sounds different from other voices and we always recall it giving us good advice, but regretfully, many times, we didn't take it. For many of us, it's after the fact, that we realize this voice was urging us to take a direction that goes against our normal; and things would have worked out for our good if only we had listened. This voice doesn't seem to care how small or how large our bank accounts are; it speaks regardless of our circumstances, status or what we deem important. It speaks to what we should eat, who we should marry, who to let our children have sleepovers with or where we should work. This voice speaks to every area of life concerning us.

Many fancy terms have been used to explain these "Something" experiences: sixth sense, ESP (extra-sensory perception), Deja vu, or intuition to name a few. That's right, experiences; you are having an experience when you hear this steering voice. Have you ever considered that you may be experiencing the "Holy Spirit"? Hold on! Don't close the book yet! Let's reason together. Why do we even say "Something"? Why not just chalk it all up to intuition and say, "My intuition told me that!" or "My sixth sense told me that!" Instead we say "Something". Why? If I may, it's because at these particular times, we know deep within that we are experiencing something different; something more than ourselves. Not convinced? Let's take a closer look at the Holy Spirit, who He is, and what His role is in our lives. The third person of our triune, God, is the Holy Spirit. That's right, person! Well, He's not a flesh and blood person like you and I, but He's considered a person, because He has emotions, a mind, and a will just like we do. Also, just as humans are communicators, so is the Holy Spirit. Honestly, what person do you know of that doesn't communicate in some form? Communication is not the only attribute we have in common with the Holy Spirit. The Holy Spirit is intelligent and searches out the deepness of

God. (1 Corinthians 2:10)

We also know that He is knowledgeable and knows the thoughts of the person it lives in as well as the Spirit of God. (1 Corinthians 2:11) Also, the personable Holy Spirit has feelings and emotions similar to ours. Ephesians 4:30 tells us that the Holy Spirit can be grieved or made sad by our actions. The Holy Spirit is God's way of relating and connecting to us.

Now, let's discuss the great work that the Holy Spirit has set out for Him. Keeping in mind that our great God, consists of God the Father, God the Son, and God the Holy Spirit, we must understand all three are one and have a common goal in mind – YOU! They are all working together, on one accord, to assist us in coming out of sin and into the marvelous light and ultimately into eternity together with Him forever. For this great plan of Salvation to be fully achieved, the Holy Spirit needed to come to usher in the next phase after Jesus paid the ultimate price with His precious blood. Look at what Jesus told His disciples:

> *But in fact, it is best for you that I go away, because if I don't, the Advocate won't come. If I do go away, then I will send him to you. John 16:7 NLT*

Although Jesus knew his disciples were about to have a panic attack when He told them He had to go away, he reassured them that it was for their benefit.

The Advocate, Jesus was talking about, is the Holy Spirit. Still not convinced? Consider this scripture:

But when the Father sends the Advocate as my representative--that is, the Holy Spirit--he will teach you everything and will remind you of everything I have told you. John 14:26 NLT

The Holy Spirit is also known as: the Comforter, Advocate, Helper, Counselor, and Teacher, just to name a few. All of these names describe the great work that the Holy Spirit has come to do in our lives. How can the Holy Spirit teach, comfort, advocate, help, or cause us to remember things if it can't speak? So, how is the Holy Spirit able to speak to us? Remember, our Godhead consists of God the Father, God the Son, and God the Holy Spirit (yes, I know I'm repeating myself). And since we were created in His image, we were also made with three parts – body, soul, and spirit. Notice the connection? Both have a spirit?

God gave us a spirit and He is able to connect with us, His Spirit, to our spirit. The Holy Spirit speaks to our spirit to guide us into all truth. It won't speak of its own words, but it will speak exactly what He heard about us, directly to us, telling us what is to come. (John 16:13) I know this is hard to take in all at once, just stay with me. The comforter has a very important role in extending the work of Jesus through us. Yes, through us! The Holy Spirit isn't just flying through the heavens like a dove, as many think. He is living inside of us, leading and guiding us, helping us to make wise choices and bringing things to our remembrance what God has said.

Consider what 1 Corinthians 6:19 NLT says, *"Don't you realize that your body is the temple of the Holy Spirit, who lives in you and was given to you by God? You do not belong to yourself."* Paul wrote this when he was dealing with the Corinthian church regarding sexual immorality. Yes, sexual immorality; if you thought you had to be perfectly righteous for the Spirit to lead you, you are wrong. Remember, God intends to save us all. Psalms 25:8 says *"Good and upright is the LORD: therefore will he teach sinners in the way".*

God the Holy Spirit is concerned about us. He wouldn't dare leave us hanging to fend for ourselves. He is fully aware of the fight we are in against evil forces. He's right there, within us, cheering us on and pointing us in the way we should go. "Something" is trying to lead us to a better life. "Something" is reminding us of the promises of God. "Something is comforting us from within with a peace that passes our natural understanding. "Something" is holding back evil forces from taking over our minds and hearts. "Something" is rearing us in the way we should go. "Something" is speaking in our inner ear and helping us to understand that we are the righteousness of God in Christ Jesus. "Something" got a hold of me and made me want to give my life to Christ. I present to you today, that "Something" is the precious Holy Spirit.

You may have heard many experts and theologians who don't believe God speaks at all today. Many want to keep God in a box and announce what He will and will not do. Isn't that strange, that people have deemed themselves God experts? I mean, He's God, He does whatever He wants. He speaks to the winds and the waves and they obey Him. Why wouldn't He speak to His most prized creation, His masterpiece - humans? God is not limited to how He speaks to us. In the scriptures you will find that He has spoken thru whirlwinds, fire, earthquakes, thunder, and prophets like Elijah. In 1 Kings 19:11-12, He spoke to Elijah in a still small voice, a whisper. Still today, God speaks to us over the pulpits across the world, on street corners, at the grocery stores using people from all walks of life to draw us closer to Him. Like He spoke to Elijah the prophet, He also speaks to us in whispers, a still small voice, directly into our spirit.

If you're not convinced or even considering that the Holy Spirit speaks, the rest of this book will be merely entertainment for you. But, "Something" tells me you're smarter than that.

PRAYER

Most gracious heavenly Father, I glorify you for who you are. While many may not understand your glorious Trinity, I thank you for making me in your triune image. Father, you thought enough of me to connect with me by way of the Holy Spirit. You love me so much, that you entrusted me with the indwelling of your Spirit, constantly leading me, guiding me, helping me, fighting for me, and loving me incessantly. Your Holy Spirit has shown me the way to live and has brought back your words to my mind when I was about to stumble. Forgive me for not recognizing your voice so many times in my life. I'm sorry for thinking it was me making decisions on my own without any help from you. I thank you for advocating for me, standing up for me and interceding for me. You never gave up on me, even those times I did wrong in your presence, you never left me. Help me to hear your voice clearly over the chaos this world brings. Speak to my heart Holy Spirit. Amen!

CHAPTER TWO

DEAF BY "NEEDS"

Philippians 4:19 But my God shall supply all your need according to his riches in glory by Christ Jesus.

As a child, my mother always made sure we visited my grandmother in Arkansas for two weeks every summer. We lived in the projects in Milwaukee, and my grandmother lived in the projects in Malvern, Arkansas. I loved visiting there. One visit, we were invited to a cousin's house that I didn't know so well. My mom was so excited, she bragged about her cousin and she couldn't wait to see them. When we pulled up to the house, my aunt Shirley was with us, I couldn't believe my eyes. The house was absolutely breathtaking. I had only seen houses like this on TV.

The grass was neat, the landscaping was so perfect, and I made sure not to step on the grass. By the time we walked inside the house, I was so amazed, I didn't want to go another step for fear I would mess something up. My mother was so happy, she was having a great time, while I was uncomfortable. I was only about 9 years old and being in this beautiful environment made me feel some kind of way. I sat quietly through the visit, antsy and ready to leave. I needed to have a conversation and I knew I couldn't have it here. When the visit was finally over, and we were walking back to the car, I couldn't hold my peace. I looked at my mom and my aunt Shirley and asked, "Why don't any of us have houses like that? Why don't we have anything nice?" I could tell my question struck them. I was angry, I didn't know people in our family could have houses like that. I wanted better for us, I just didn't know how to make it happen.

"You can take this city Kara, they will never see you coming," one of my friends was telling me as we turned up our drinks. It was the weekend and drinking, loud music, clubbing, or just sitting around jabbering of ways to get quick money was a ritual. No one ever suggested going to college and getting an education to get that dream job. It was always how can we hustle to get money now? Once the liquor wore off, the get quick money schemes usually wore off with it. This time it was different. I could hear a voice urging me on. "This plan makes sense Kara, most people you know already smoke weed; it'll be easy." The voice was right, I knew where the drug houses were in my neighborhood. "You don't need to tell anybody, just do it. Your friends are not really serious anyway, but you, are about business." The plan was set. The voice laid out every detail, I even knew who my loyal customers would be. It was a solid plan and I would be safe, the voice reassured me.

I parked my car two blocks from my mother's house, the drug house was two blocks south of her place, so I was now four blocks away from the drug house. I didn't want my mom to be aware of anything in case something went wrong. The voice assured me this was best. My mom was always listening intently in case her and my sister had to hit the floor dodging bullets with no name. "We're just being extra careful, nothing is going to go wrong", the voice guaranteed me. I made sure the safety was off on the 22 caliber that was in my pocket and I began walking. I was starting to second guess myself on the long four block walk to my possible doom. Every argument against what I was doing seemed to be countered with an argument in favor. There was a literal battle inside my head. I listened to both sides as I got closer to the house; I still had time to turn around. My heart was pounding so loudly, my ears were moving. The voice that wanted me to go through with this wicked plan reminded me of how I was struggling as a single mom and barely able to buy food and pay bills.

That was it for me, I rang the doorbell. Someone had already seen me from the window, casing me out. I hope they don't think I'm a cop. "They won't," the voice snapped. I tried to put on a serious grin (whatever that looks like) as the door opened.

I knew the guy standing at the door. "What's up,

what you doin' here?" He looked confused.

"I need an ounce of weed, I mean an onion." He laughed out loud like he had just heard the best joke of the century. He knew I was an amateur, I couldn't use the slang right.

He gestured to another guy sitting in the living room, "Hey dude, she wants a onion." The other guy picked up on the humor and laughed with him. I didn't know the other guy who had joined in mocking me. I scolded the voice that led me here. "I knew this was a stupid idea, even they know I shouldn't be here!"

"Relax," the voice comforted, "They are just surprised, you got this. Now get that stupid look off your face and look serious". I tried to look offended and hard so they could see I didn't get the joke.

The other guy in the room said, "Man, she's serious." The guy standing at the door stopped smiling.

He stared at me and said, "So, you wanna get in the game"?

"Something like that," I replied. He walked away, never inviting me in, which was good because the voice told me to never leave the door. The other guy in the living room never took his eyes off me, it made me uncomfortable. I stood waiting at the door, attempting to look unafraid, but was actually terrified. When the guy I knew walked back into the living room, the other guy whispered something to him.

"Naw, she good, her mom's live around the corner from here".

My spine got weak, they knew where my mother lives. I was trying to prevent this. I was hoping they couldn't see me trembling. He walked over to me and handed me the "onion", and I handed him the money. "Make sure you see me when it's time to re-up."

"I will," I declared as I darted for the porch. I couldn't get down the front steps fast enough. My ears were pulling back as I walked away, I could feel stares piercing me from behind. My eyesight changed, I could see so clearly it was as though I had night vision. I suddenly felt athletic. I didn't realize I was running. All of my senses were heightened, I never felt more alive. I could hear the blood rushing through my veins, I felt euphoric. The voice led me back to my car in a different direction, I began darting through yards and alleys. Now was not the time to care about stepping on someone's grass or being on someone's property. Adrenaline had lifted me off my feet and I was back at my car before I knew it.

I looked around and held tight to the gun that was still in my pocket, making sure I wasn't followed. I jumped in my car and drove away. I began laughing, "Whew!! I couldn't believe it. I could get used to this feeling. The voice was satisfied, everything worked out as it had planned. The voice had big plans for me, it told me I could trust it. It told me how I could get out of the hood and live a better life. It reassured me I wouldn't have to do this for long and that there was so much more it had in store for me. I couldn't stop smiling. I had actually done it, I felt accomplished. Now I understand why others do it. It wasn't just the money, it was the rush. I didn't go back to my mother's house that night to pick up my kids. I didn't want to try to explain this new high and I was having a hard time calming down from what I had just experienced. I called some friends over to celebrate, only they didn't know why we were celebrating.

The voice warned me not to tell anyone what I had done. As far as they knew, it was just hanging out. The next day, the voice and I had to start working on the next phase of the plan – my customer base. I called one of my girls over, who I knew smoked weed religiously. The voice told me she would be my first and most loyal customer. Something in me made me feel guilty. "She's a mother, she's your friend," something said to me. I had been knowing her since high school, I had much love for her. But the voice convinced me that I was only going to be providing what she was already getting from someone else. I thought about how smoothly everything had worked out the night before and I shook that guilty feeling off.

When she walked in and saw the weed spread out on the table, she screamed. "What the h… is this"? Her eyes were big, and I laughed hysterically. I wanted so badly to tell her of the experience from the night before.

"Roll one up," I told her. The doorbell rung, I wasn't expecting anybody. We looked at each other puzzlingly. I looked out of the window from my upper unit and saw a car that I was very familiar with. It was Wayne's blue Cutlass. He didn't even call to say he was coming by. Wayne and I went to high school together and had been talking on the phone lately. There were some strong feelings between us, but I could tell he was holding back and so I did too. It was strange that he just popped up like this, he had never done this before; our relationship hadn't advanced to the "pop up at your door" level.

I opened the door and he was standing there smiling like something was on his mind – me. I returned the look, I was always happy to see him. He was different from other guys. I stood there looking at him in his Levi jeans and jacket, smelling good. I invited him in forgetting all about the weed that was spread all over my living room table and my friend that was rolling up a joint. When Wayne walked into the living room and saw what was going on, his smile turned to shock and then to anger. I'll never forget the look on his face. He quickly walked to the table, scooped up the weed and began stomping towards the back of my unit, right to the bathroom. My friend and I both knew what he was going to do, flush it down the toilet. We were screaming at him, pulling on him. It was as if he became an iron bulldozer, we couldn't stop him. The next thing we heard was the toilet flush. I stood frozen in unbelief. He turned to me and said, "I will not deal with anyone who does this!" He had a cold look in his eyes as he stared into mine for what seemed like an eternity.

Silence filled the room after he belted out his ultimatum. I was in shock and confused at what had just happened. Something in me was shouting with joy. Something else in me was angry and screaming "Who does he think he is?" He turned around, bolted down the stairs of my unit, got in his blue Cutlass and sped off. We heard his tires burn rubber and we remained in silence. My girl still standing in bewilderment said, "That man loves you." I became so embarrassed, so ashamed. I had never felt like this before. I had never seen this kind of reaction from anyone out of the neighborhood before. Confusion filled me and I just wanted to be alone to think. The voice tried to tell me I just needed to forget about Wayne and focus on our plan, but somehow, I was able to shut it down. I didn't want to hear anything it had to say. I was too busy wondering how Wayne's mindset was different from everybody else's. We went to the same school and lived in the same neighborhood. "He thinks he's better than you," the voice chided. I didn't listen. Instead, I began to see the danger I had put myself and my family in. I was done with the voice that had gotten me into this disaster. It went away, but only for a short time.

Your story may be different from mine, but I'm sure you can still relate on some level. When needs turn into wants, and then wants to turn into greed, things can go wrong very quickly. God promises to supply all of our need according to His riches in glory by Christ Jesus. *(Philippians 4:19)* If we look at this promise closely, it is both restrictive and unlimited. When I see the word "all" in Philippians 4:19, I understand that whatever I need, no matter how much I need and at any given point, God will provide not just half or some of what I need, but "All." His resources are unlimited. However, when I see the singular word "need" that tells me I shouldn't expect a surplus of what He is providing, only what is sufficient or needed at that particular time. He's not going to give out more than we can handle. What an awesome and thoughtful Father He is! Any parent worth his or her salt should be able to understand and appreciate this concept.

If you give a child too much, they become spoiled and unappreciative; they may even throw a temper tantrum if they don't get what they want. So God says, I'll supply what you need, all of what you need, but I'll restrict it as I see fit. What God has for us, all of His riches in glory, is too enormous for us to handle; He had to put some structure around this awesome promise. Here is the structure: "by Christ Jesus" (I just got excited). God will meet "all of our need" on any scale; the scope of that scale is based on our level of relationship with Christ Jesus.

Now, let's test this concept against my life, (since I was so transparent at the beginning of this chapter).

I wanted an enlarged territory in my younger days, however, I went about it all wrong. I looked at my surroundings and couldn't see past the poverty, drugs and crime that I witnessed daily. I was going to church but didn't pray and ask God for His assistance to help me get out of the horrible pit I was in. Instead, I allowed my environment to dictate how I would go after what I wanted. My true needs were being met. I had a job, low paying, but still a job. I had a car, it wasn't always running, but it got me where I needed to be. I was able to pay my bills, I didn't have extra money to spend but I was able to take care of what was necessary. Can you see how God met my "need" and restricted His overflow of blessings toward me due to the lifestyle I was living? I can! He kept His promise to me; I reneged. I couldn't get to the next level for two reasons: I wasn't grateful for the blessings I was receiving, and I didn't have a real relationship with Christ Jesus.

I had so much to be grateful for. I was young, living on my own and able to care for my, at that time, two children. I had a loving mother, sister, and family. I was so busy looking at what I didn't have, that I completely overlooked what I did have. Jesus warned, *"Watch out! Be on your guard against all kinds of greed; a man's life does not consist in the abundance of his possessions." (Luke 12:15 NIV)* I wasn't on watch or on guard against greed. To me living an abundant life was all about possessions and nothing to do with a real relationship with Christ. I allowed the voice of my needs, to be louder than the Holy Spirit that was directing me. When I think back over that time in my life, I can remember the Holy Spirit speaking to me, warning me and showing me a better way. But my flesh was louder and it gave place to the enemy to come in and take over.

I didn't know Christ Jesus for myself, I had only heard of Him through others and movies. I did attend church, but I wasn't able to hear the word with my heart to even begin developing a relationship. My flesh was so strong, that my spirit was weak, but God was still good to me. Not only did He meet my "need," He gave me a way to escape from the horrible choice I had made. Look at what I Corinthians 10:13 says, *"There hath no temptation taken you but such as is common to man: but God is faithful, who will not suffer you to be tempted above that ye are able; but will with the temptation also make a way to escape, that ye may be able to bear it"*. God is definitely a promise keeper. He provided a way of escape when I was headed for sure destruction. I never would have guessed Wayne would show up at my house that day unannounced; it was so out of the ordinary. I asked him some time after, what made him just pop up at my house, his response, "I don't know, 'Something', told me I should stop by". There is that same "Something" that was working to steer me; it led Wayne that day to help me escape a fate that would have set me on a path to destruction and one that God had not planned for me.

Satan has always used the voice of human needs to tempt and distract people from hearing God's voice and prevent them from walking into their destiny. Even Jesus was subjected to the enemy's temptation tactics during His time here on earth. Immediately after Jesus had been baptized by John the Baptist (Matthew 3:13-16), He was faced with the devil's enticements in the wilderness. Let's see how Jesus handled temptation by Satan in Matthew 4 NLT.

Then Jesus was led by the Spirit into the wilderness to be tempted there by the devil. 2 For forty days and forty nights he fasted and became very hungry. 3 During that time the devil came and said to him, "If you are the Son of God, tell these stones to become loaves of bread." 4 But Jesus told him, "No! The Scriptures say,

'People do not live by bread alone, but by every word that comes from the mouth of God.'

5 Then the devil took him to the holy city, Jerusalem, to the highest point of the Temple, 6 and said, "If you are the Son of God, jump off! For the Scriptures say, 'He will order his angels to protect you. And they will hold you up with their hands

So you won't even hurt your foot on a stone.'" 7 Jesus responded, "The Scriptures also say, 'You must not test the Lord your God.'"

8 Next the devil took him to the peak of a very high mountain and showed him all the kingdoms of the world and their glory. 9 "I will give it all to you," he said, "if you will kneel down and worship me." 10

"Get out of here, Satan," Jesus told him. "For the Scriptures say, 'You must worship the Lord your God and serve only him."

11 Then the devil went away, and angels came and took care of Jesus.

I would like to point out that Jesus was led by the Spirit into the wilderness to be tempted by the devil. This was orchestrated by God the Father so that Jesus could identify with us as a human being and we could understand that it is possible to not give in to temptation with the help of Jesus. Hebrews 2:18 NIV *Because he himself suffered when he was tempted, he is able to help those who are being tempted.*

Notice how the devil waited until Jesus was physically weak and hungry before he began his temptation strategies on him; he doesn't fight fair. Can you imagine how hungry Jesus must have been after fasting for 40 days? Satan started with a physical need to tempt Jesus with since He was in human form and knew he was hungry; so he told Jesus to turn a stone into bread. The devil is still using the same tactics today. Hunger pangs can be so painful that they scream for us to get food by any means necessary. Humans need food to survive, and if you don't have food on your table or in your cabinets, means to obtain it can become problematic.

The enemy will coax many people to fall into stealing, robbing, or even killing to get food when there is none in sight. But Jesus fought back with the word of God. *But he answered and said, It is written, Man shall not live by bread alone, but by every word that proceedeth out of the mouth of God. (Matthew 4:4)* Jesus recited Deuteronomy 8:3, letting the devil know what we all must ultimately learn, and that is God's word is superior to any carnal sustenance we could ever nourish ourselves with. The devil continued with his scheme by now taking Jesus to the pinnacle of the temple and telling him to jump. *And saith unto him, If thou be the Son of God, cast thyself down: for it is written, He shall give his angels charge concerning thee: and in their hands they shall bear thee up, lest at any time thou dash thy foot against a stone. (Matthew 4:6 NLT)* Yes, the devil quoted a Holy Scripture, Psalms 91:12, on our Lord and Savior, twisting it to convince Him to test God; but Jesus didn't fall for it. Jesus gave Him an uppercut with, *"It is written again, Thou shalt not tempt the Lord thy God" from Deuteronomy 6:16.*

This battle is getting serious; now Satan pulls out his infamous play on wealth. When Jesus walked the earth, He did not live like a rich man, but He was rather poor. Later in the Bible we learn that Jesus didn't even have a place to live. But Jesus replied, *"Foxes have dens to live in, and birds have nests, but the Son of Man has no place even to lay his head." (Luke 9:58 NLT)* I guess that is why the devil thought he should tempt Jesus with riches and power.

Again, the devil taketh him up into an exceeding high mountain, and sheweth him all the kingdoms of the world, and

the glory of them;
9 And saith unto him, All these things will I give thee, if thou wilt fall down and worship me. (Matthew 4:8-9) The devil has wanted to be worshipped ever since he fell from glory. Offering Jesus a quick seat to an earthly kingdom and avoiding the cross; I don't think so Satan. The first Adam may have turned over his authority to you, but certainly not Jesus, the second Adam.

Get out of here, Satan," Jesus told him. "For the Scriptures say, You must worship the Lord your God and serve only him." (Matthew 4:10 NLT) This battle went three rounds and ended with a 1-2 knockout combination. Jesus clearly had enough of Satan's foolishness and told him where to go, "Get out of here Satan". Then he sealed the command with a quote from *Deuteronomy 6:13 You must fear the LORD your God and serve him. When you take an oath, you must use only his name.* The enemy tried to make Jesus misuse His power and authority for selfish reasons. Did he really think Jesus could be anything like him? The technique Jesus used against Satan's tactics is fail proof and if we use it we too can be successful against the enemy's tempting voice. Learning scripture is critical in this battle against evil. The more scripture we speak against the enemy, the more powerful we become.

The Word of God has the power to save our souls and cleanse us from evil. *So get rid of all the filth and evil in your lives, and humbly accept the word God has planted in your hearts, for it has the power to save your souls. But don't just listen to God's word. You must do what it says. Otherwise, you are only fooling yourselves. (James 1:21-22 NLT)* It is time for us to stand up against the evil voice of Satan that constantly tempts and accuses us. We must be sober and alert, on watch at all times for the enemy's devices. Putting on the whole armour of God, so that we can stand against the wiles of the devil. James 4:7 Submit yourselves therefore to God. Resist the devil, and he will flee from you. Let's say it together, **"Get out of here Satan"**.

PRAYER

Most gracious heavenly Father, you are Jehovah Jireh, my provider. The earth is yours and the fullness thereof. Your riches extend far beyond anything I could ever imagine. You are the source of all things. You met my need even when I didn't deserve it. You have been a good Father to me, teaching me gratefulness by restricting your blessings in my immaturity. You didn't allow Satan to destroy me while I was so deep in sin that I couldn't hear your precious Holy Spirit leading me to right paths. Forgive me for allowing deceitful thoughts and vain imaginations to creep in. I thank you for being patient with me. You kept just enough distance from me so you could still protect me and keep a watchful eye over me even while I was trapped in iniquity. Your grace and mercy followed me through wicked schemes and despair. My relationship with you is more valuable than anything I could ever gain on this earth. Your word is the cleanser and protector of my soul. I'm living proof that seeking you first will result in you adding things to me. My life is yours, you are my abundance. I glorify your Holy name. Amen!

CHAPTER THREE

DEAF BY DRY PLACES

Matthew 12:43 When the unclean spirit is gone out of a man, he walketh through dry places, seeking rest, and findeth none.
44 Then he saith, I will return into my house from whence I came out; and when he is come, he findeth it empty, swept, and garnished.
45 Then goeth he, and taketh with himself seven other spirits more wicked than himself, and they enter in and dwell there: and the last state of that man is worse than the first. Even so shall it be also unto this wicked generation.

Demons love dry places! There is no place like home to a demon unless it is dry and void of the Holy Spirit. I should know; I provided dry shelters to these destructive forces for many years of my life. My spiritual ear was packed tight with smoldering dry sands; damaging my spiritual hearing and obliterating any chance of a divine message getting through to me. Many times I gave these evil spirits eviction notices; (the guilt and shame of being an unclean dwelling place often got the best of me and made me want to clean house). So, I held my head up, pushed my pride to the side and walked to the front of the church during the altar call. I sincerely confessed my sins and declared I wanted to be a new creature in Christ. The good news is that the invaders had to go and try to find somewhere else to dwell. The bad news is that all the other dry places were taken so the evil ones hung around my premises until I let them right back in, and I usually did.

There I was, in a vicious cycle of renting dry space to demons who were hoping to ultimately destroy me. Jesus told us all about the dry places cycle in Matthew 12. He described these dry places as empty, swept, and garnished. It is interesting that Jesus used these words to describe the dry places as they are all synonyms for each other meaning empty. Basically, Jesus is saying these dry places are empty, emptier, and emptiest. Every time you renege on your repentance, you become drier each time until it is too late. It is almost impossible for a spiritually dry human to hear the voice of the Lord; the emptiness is spiritually earsplitting. Look closer at what Jesus is saying; there are different stages of emptiness that causes a deafening dryness.

The initial empty stage is having a void of what is necessary to connect with God the Holy Spirit. This is the same Holy Spirit from chapter one that we often call His voice "Something". He is the third person of the Holy Trinity to be exact and He is just what we need to have a relationship with God Our Father. He whispers to us and writes words in our hearts; if we would dare allow. He works like a well-oiled machine in a temple that is moist with His Word. Keepers of His commandments make an awesome dwelling place for Him. He is always thrilled to lead, guide, speak, and intercede on behalf of His gracious and loving vessel. Add in consistent prayer life, and He is thriving while energizing His host to be the best image of God that they can possibly be. Now, take all of that away, and you get a house that has closed all the shutters on the promised Comforter.

The windows have been painted black to darken out the "Son". The water supply from the source has been cut off and the pipes are starting to rust. The choking, stifled spirit within is weakened and struggling to get a connection through, but all to no avail. The walls inside of this dry vessel are layered in soundproof cement, blocking out any chance of hearing a word from the well of everlasting life. The evil force inside has started dismantling the connection with the Holy Spirit. The inward turmoil begins to take a toll and the vessel begins to express it on the outside. Where this host use to have a passion for serving, has now become disgruntled and feeling like their time is being wasted.

The thought of another meeting or rehearsal causes more frustration than anticipation. The zeal once had to serve God's people has now turned into indifference. Serving now feels like the bondage of obligation. Work is no longer committed to the Lord, but is rushed and filled with annoyance. "When is this going to be over? I'm sick of dealing with these church people!" Patience is short-circuiting and the light of Christ is starting to dim. The host is having a spiritual blackout. The chatter of demons is getting louder and suddenly it is getting easier and easier to be offended. Wicked thoughts, evil imaginations are flooding the host's mind. It's hard for this vessel to focus while praying. The evil minion on the inside is getting cozier now. He is even sending out invites to 7 other spirits "more wicked" than himself to ensure they have a home as dry as the Arizona heat in August. While there is still hope in this stage, this is just the beginning of the deafening emptiness that Jesus warned about.

As if the empty stage was not bad enough, brace yourself for the swept stage. I always imagine a demon holding a wicked evil-looking broom and violently sweeping away at anything Holy that comes near the boundaries of the place he calls home. How many times have you sat in church and paid more attention to distractions than the word that was going forth? The preacher is passionately proclaiming the blood of Jesus over your life, but thoughts of what you are going to eat after service are shouting louder than the preacher's voice. Somehow the cries of a baby are more attention-grabbing than the Word being declared. Commotions seem to start coming out of nowhere. From the people behind you chattering, to the microphones squealing, your head is on a swivel looking backward and forwards, left to right; everywhere, but at the pulpit where words of life are being made transparent.

Even while trying to go through the motions, the dryness has settled in and that same demon that claims you to be his home is standing ready to scream louder than any word the preacher can shout, or the choir can sing. Here is some breaking news for you; this is not an accident and I can prove it. Jesus warned us about this in the parable of the sower: *Mark 4:15 KJV And these are they by the wayside, where the word is sown; but when they have heard, Satan cometh immediately, and taketh away the word that was sown in their hearts.* In this passage, Jesus was standing on a boat as He taught by the sea. He used a parable of farming because that is what the people were familiar with during that time. He was explaining how when a farmer plants seeds, the seeds fall onto different types of soil. Look at how James Merritt explains the various soils:

> *"Jesus describes the first kind of soil as "the path."*
>
> *In Palestine, people would walk through fields and take the same path each day. As they traveled, they would trample down the grass and the ground would become rock-hard. The seed could not get into this type of soil. It could get on the ground, but not into the ground.*
>
> *The second type of soil was rocky soil. Much of Israel is limestone and bedrock that is covered with a thin layer of soil. While the first soil was soil where the seed could*

not get in, this is soil where the seed could not get down.

In the thorny soil, however, the seed takes root, but the plant is hindered from growing. It can't get out. The Word of God is choked out by financial prosperity and worldly possessions.

These are the people who hear the Word of God and say they want to follow the Son of God, but the golf course, the lake house, the extra money, the bigger paycheck, and the corporate ladder keep getting in the way. Getting and keeping these things is more important than following Jesus.

There is, though, a fourth type of soil. Jesus describes it as a heart receptive to God's Word. This is the heart that bears fruit. Some people will say yes and mean it and bear fruit for God's kingdom."
(Merritt, 101-102) [1]

What is important for us to understand is that the seed is the Word of God. The seed was not the problem, but rather the different soils the seeds landed on: wayside (pathway), rocky places, among thorns and good ground. All seed, the Word of God, is good and has the potential to bear fruit; it is the soil, or the heart, which determines how deep it takes root or if it roots at all. The enemy is standing and patiently waiting to pluck the word that was sown right out of the heart. The evil intruder knows very well that if those life-giving words get through, he has to move out and try to find another dry home. He never underestimates the power of God's words and knows that once heard all of the dryness will become saturated with living waters.

Satan and his dryads are very familiar with Isaiah 58:11 all too well and are deathly afraid of it: Isaiah 58:11 NLT *The LORD will guide you continually, giving you water when you are dry and restoring your strength. You will be like a well-watered garden, like an ever-flowing spring.* Yes, this is a promise from God to guide you and keep you strengthened and watered with His Holy Spirit. But we must fight the evil forces that have barricaded themselves within, struggling to keep a roof over their heads. This emptier stage of dryness follows one right out of the church doors and into their cars, homes, and jobs. The enemy knows that the word of God is inspiring and gives hope to the one who hears it, so he must stay on the attack.

I can remember being in this stage. I was not sure if I even wanted to go to church any longer. I was starting to feel like there was no benefit. It seemed like every time I took one step forward, I was pushed back two. I was becoming emptier. I felt distant from God and I was not growing spiritually. I felt discouraged and the burdens of life weighed on me heavily. Memories of my mom teaching me to recite Psalm 23 would pop in my mind and I would begin to say it out loud. "The Lord is my...." The phone would ring, and it was someone calling to go out to eat or to a movie.

My wicked trespasser had to do something quick to sweep Psalms 23 out of my mind; knowing very well those powerful verses could definitely spark a connection through the darkness. I was going to church on Sundays to keep up appearances but then decided that it was no longer worth it. Assembling myself with other believers had become a serious waste of time. Why go to church when I could be working more hours on my job or solidifying my social life? I was no longer receiving the word of God and starting to feel the empty side effects: lack of faith, hopeless, no guidance or direction, and unanswered prayers. The enemy had swept scriptures from my heart that showed me how critical receiving the Word of God is.

FAITH
Romans 10:17 KJV So then faith comes by hearing, and hearing by the word of God.

HOPE
Romans 15:4 KJV For whatsoever things were written aforetime were written for our learning, that we through patience and comfort of the scriptures might have hope.

Psalm 119:50 KJV This is my comfort in my affliction: for thy word hath quickened me.

GUIDANCE AND DIRECTION
Psalms 119:105 NLT Your word is a lamp to guide my feet and a light for my path.

Proverbs 6:23 KJV For the commandment is a

lamp; and the law is light; and reproofs of instruction are the way of life

ANSWERED PRAYERS

John 15:7 NLT But if you remain in me and my words remain in you, you may ask for anything you want, and it will be granted!

1 John 5:14 NLT And we are confident that he hears us whenever we ask for anything that pleases him.

1 John 3:22 KJV And whatsoever we ask, we receive of him, because we keep his commandments, and do those things that are pleasing in his sight.

I did not realize it, but I was being swept. I would try to pray, but my words felt empty and I was not able to stay focused long enough to complete it. There is that evil broom, sweeping away frantically at every thought of righteousness. The demon's goals and only concern are keeping his current home tidy and dry so there is no way he can be kicked out and have to go through the trouble of starting all over again. My soul was being held hostage and I did not have enough Word in me to understand that my ransom had already been paid in precious blood.

There is still hope in this swept stage. The vessel is not completely dry yet, but it is an uphill battle. The spirit that remains is starving, grieved, but not dead and is still fighting to bring things to the vessel's remembrance to help remind them of who they are and whose they are. The last stage, garnished, is brutal. The evil companion now has bragging rights and has secured his name on the lease of the host's soul. The devil no longer has to even bother about trying to pluck God's word out of hearts; the flesh is now doing it on its own.

The heart is hardened against the word of God. Jesus said, in this state, the person is worse than the first stages. *(Matthew 12:45)* A heart without the Word of God is only able to produce from the evil treasury that is being stockpiled within. Matthew 12:25 NLT Jesus said, *"A good person produces good things from the treasury of a good heart, and an evil person produces evil things from the treasury of an evil heart.* The image of God is all but swept away from the vessel; there is no resemblance. The appearance of the true and living God is replaced by the image of the "father of lies", "the impersonator", "and the accuser". These dry ones no longer put their trust in God, but in themselves and their own abilities.

Righteousness and God's moral code is no longer evident in this phase. Forgiveness, compassion, and love have all been traded in for revenge, lustful pleasures, and worldly gain. The dryness has caused a spiritual ear infection, to the point of going deaf. The flesh is screaming so loudly in this stage that the way to salvation is not recognizable. God's escape routes from your failures, storms, and formed weapons seem to have vanished and wise decisions are far out of reach. Believing that there is actually a God who loves and cares is a fallacy in this state. Being grateful for the finished work on the Cross and accepting Jesus as Lord and savior is not even on this person's radar.

The devil and his dryads work tirelessly to get humans in the final destructive arid state. In addition to not having the word of God, faith or a prayer life, you are now void of what you need to receive salvation causing one to be emptiest or garnished. The spirit is deeply malnourished and weakened at this point. Like an expensive meal at an exclusive restaurant, you are garnished and beautified by the standards of the world. You are only capable of following the desires of the dry sinful nature that have made a resting place for demons. Your fate has been told for generations in Galatians 5:19-20 NLT *When you follow the desires of your sinful nature, the results are very clear: sexual immorality, impurity, lustful pleasures, 20 idolatry, sorcery, hostility, quarreling, jealousy, outbursts of anger, selfish ambition, dissension, division, 21 envy, drunkenness, wild parties, and other sins like these. Let me tell you again, as I have before, that anyone living that sort of life will not inherit the Kingdom of God.* That's right, in this state, you lose your heavenly inheritance. God has turned you over to a reprobate mind, to do with your devices as you wish. You have turned away from the "Truth" to do the things that are convenient to your flesh. This last state is worse than the first.

I am so thankful I did not get to that last state of being garnished and ultimately separated from my Lord and Savior Jesus Christ. God had to allow some very painful events to happen in my life to get my attention; He took drastic measures. Tragedies struck that shook me to my core. One night I turned on the television and there was my husband on the news being accused of criminal activity. I was stunned as I realized the man I had known since the age of 9, I really did not know at all. He had a totally separate life from me; one that I had no clue about. I was in shock. I tried to stick it out with him, telling him I would do whatever it took to save our marriage, even getting a second job. A short time later, I came home from work to find he had left.

Normally, I would have reacted in a way that would have given him reason to call me deranged, but another tragedy struck right away that needed my attention. My mother's health was failing. I had to stay nights at her house while my sister and I took care of her. I had to table my broken marriage to nurse my mom. I was feeling nauseated all the time. How can both of these events be happening simultaneously? The sadness I felt was indescribable, there was nothing I could do to make it better. My mother passed away... Just when I thought life could not get any worse, friends walked out of my life for reasons that did not make any sense. Others followed suit for no reason at all. I dare not put any of this on my sister, she had a new husband and baby to focus on. I was all alone and this is exactly where God wanted me.

I had hit rock bottom and only God could pick

me up out of this pit. I was in my own specially created wilderness; designed just for me. "God! Please help me!" It was like those words had touched the hem of His garment and He turned to say "Who touched me?" My soul was thirsting for living waters. I understand how David felt when he was in his own wilderness experience: *O God, you are my God; I earnestly search for you. My soul thirsts for you; my whole body longs for you in this parched and weary land where there is no water. 2 I have seen you in your sanctuary and gazed upon your power and glory. 3 Your unfailing love is better than life itself; how I praise you! (Psalm 63:1 NLT)* I began to praise God the way I knew how, singing:

My soul, loves Jesus. My soul, loves Jesus. My soul, loves Jesus, bless His name. He's a wonder, to my soul. He's a wonder, to my soul. He's a wonder, to my soul. Bless His name.

The spirit led me to pick up my Bible and brought scriptures back to my remembrance. Scriptures that I thought had been swept away. *But the word of the Lord remains forever. And that word is the Good News that was preached to you. (I Peter 1:25 NLT)* I realized at that moment, the Lord was with me the entire time. I was never alone. I made a vow to never be dry and empty of the Word of God again.

PRAYER

Most gracious heavenly Father, I praise you from the depths of my soul. When I was in my wilderness, in a dry and empty state, you had a plan in mind the entire time to bring me out. You allowed me to see myself and the error of my ways. You kept a watch over me while I was in my distress. You did not allow the enemy to completely devour me and separate me from you. I am so grateful for the Word you planted deep down inside of my heart so that the enemy could not find it to pluck it out. You refused to let me be garnished and in a worse state. Your unfailing love for me, kept me during my darkest hour. My heart is swollen with thanksgiving and gratefulness for all you have done. Your Word will forever water my soul with living waters. My soul loves you and I will forever praise your holy and righteous name.

CHAPTER FOUR

DEAF BY BAD LOVE

"Something told me it was over
When I saw you and her talkin'
Something deep down in my soul said, 'Cry, girl'
When I saw you and that girl walkin' out
Whoo, I would rather, I would rather go blind, boy
Than to see you walk away from me, child, no
Whoo, so you see, I love you so much
That I don't wanna watch you leave me, baby
Most of all, I just don't, I just don't wanna be free, no"

Etta James rang out those lyrics in her soulful song, "I'd Rather Go Blind", recorded in 1967. Those stanzas are the perfect example of a screaming flesh roaring louder than the "Something" that was trying to prepare her for the truth. If we look at these lyrics closely, we know that she saw what was happening with her own eyes, no one told her about the "other woman". Next, she gets a deep revelation down in her soul; that yes what you are seeing is true so start your mourning now to begin your healing process; your eyes are not deceiving you.

What comes next is mind-boggling, her flesh won't allow her to accept what she sees with her eyes and what she knows in her soul. Her flesh wants to stay a slave to a deceptive relationship that is not healthy for her but feels good to her. Even worse, her flesh is willing to go blind to look the other way, to continue in the elusive relationship. How many of us have been in this situation before? I know I have, more than I'd like to admit. These lyrics resonated within me and it captures what many of us have gone through at some point in our lives. I can't say what those lyrics meant to Etta James, but when I heard them, they struck cords within me and as I related with them all too well.

The words to this song connected with me and forced me to take a look at past relationships and how I allowed my flesh to boom louder than what I knew deep inside. The first few words of the song are what stood out to me most, "Something told me it was over". Now that I look back over my life, I can remember the times I had feelings or thoughts; and yes, even a voice in my head that told me danger was ahead. My flesh didn't want to accept the truth.

I dreamed of leaving the Parklawn projects; I wanted the American dream: a husband, children, and that white picket fence in front of my house. At the age of 16, I started dating one of our church's musicians. Everyone thought it was fate since we were the youth bride and groom in a Tom Thumb wedding as children. I fell in love, even though he was a few years older than me, and we married when I was 17. He joined the Army and we moved to New York where he was stationed at Fort Drum. We had plans of me going to college and we would work hard to obtain our dreams; only the fantasy didn't last long.

Quickly, he became cruel and then the physical abuse started. I couldn't believe this was happening to me. I was young, I needed him to be nurturing and protective, but instead he was my tormentor. I won't describe everything that happened between us, out of respect for my son. I had no family, no friends, no one to turn to in New York; he controlled my entire life. I could only call my mother on Sundays for 30 minutes, and my calls were usually monitored. I couldn't call my best friend, or anyone else. He reviewed the phone bills to make sure I wasn't on the phone during the week, but he could call whoever and whenever he wanted.

Any furniture that his parents had given us, I wasn't allowed to sit on. Some nights I was locked out of the bedroom and had to sleep on the couch. "You're not even that pretty, I've had plenty girlfriends who look better than you," he'd often say. On those days he wouldn't come home at all, it was a relief. I thought once I became pregnant, things would get better; it got worse. I had my baby boy and my dog, a Pitbull named Lady, they were my comfort. One day he came in from being gone for over a week and was on a rampage about the dog being on the couch.

Then, he grabbed my son from my arms and I lost it. For the first time, I fought back with everything I had. Shortly after, he decided that he needed a break from us. He came home with a Greyhound bus ticket to Milwaukee and said that our son and I had to leave. I was devastated. I begged and cried to stay, but he was cold and unmoving. I wanted to be married, I didn't want to fail. I thought, marriage was supposed to be forever. He ripped my wedding ring off as well as the gold chain from around my neck. It was cold and in the middle of winter. "The only thing you can take with you is this coat and a baby bag."

He drove us to the bus station and when I turned around to say goodbye, he had disappeared. I felt like my heart had been ripped from my chest. I walked around the bus terminal, hopeless and defeated with no luggage. On one of the stops, I called my mother to let her know I was headed home, but he had already called her. I tried to sound happy and told her it was just a visit. She knew something wasn't right, but she was more excited about my son and me coming home than anything else.

It felt so good to be home, back in the projects with my mom and sister. I had peace. I never told my mom what married life was like for me back in New York. I didn't want to talk about it, I was enjoying being home. I tried calling him a few times but he never answered. 2 weeks went by, and he called. "I'm ready for you and the baby to come home now." I held the phone in silence. I didn't want to go back, but I said "OK".

I began to cry and my mother asked me what was wrong. I said, "Mama, I can't go back!" I didn't even have to tell her all of the horrible things I had been through, her response was simply, "Then don't go back!" That's all I needed to hear… I filed for divorce! I was trying to put the pieces of my life back together. I contacted my friends and explained my disappearance from them and why I hadn't called or written.

I found a job and started feeling better about myself. I ran into a friend that I grew up with in the projects. We were close growing up and I was glad to see him. He had left for the Marines after high school and I hadn't seen him in a few years. We spent time catching up and it wasn't long before we went from just being friends to a romantic relationship. We had a lot in common. We both were newly divorced and came back to Milwaukee shattered. I thought he was just what I needed, we knew each other so well. I also thought I was just what he needed too, boy was I wrong.

He needed me, but I wasn't enough, he needed more. Slowly I began to suspect other women. We broke up several times, on again, off again. After years of breaking up and having other failed relationships, we got married. He convinced me he had changed, and I desperately needed to believe it. I wanted a husband and I told myself that he was easy to fall in love with because I had known him for so many years. It wasn't long after we said our vows that the suspicions started up again. I couldn't believe it, but then again, I could. I tried to ignore the warning signs, I didn't want to get divorced again. Besides, my true love Wayne, who God used to save me from a life of devastation, had gotten married to someone else in our time apart. I was still going to my old church and was active in the choir, but to spend time with my husband I drank alcohol, partied, and traveled with him, trying to make sure he didn't have time to cheat, but he always found a way.

Together, we had four children, two from me, one from him and one together. We had a nice home, which I had purchased before we married, but I still found myself miserable. One night I came home from work after picking the kids up from my mother's, and I noticed the house was dark and silent. My husband was usually home before me. I told the kids to stand in the kitchen while I looked through the house to make sure everything was alright. I noticed his clothes were missing. I went to the basement and all of the furniture was gone. We hadn't been robbed by a stranger, he left us. No letter, no call, no nothing. He was all set up in another house with another woman and there was nothing I could do about it. Actually, there was nothing I wanted to do about it! He had shown me who he was so many times; it took him walking out on me and my children for me to finally believe it.

I was done! "No more marriage for me," I declared. It was too hard trusting someone with my heart; they trample all over it. I told God that I was done and that the only way I would marry again is if He, God, told me himself. I needed new surroundings; I needed to put away old thinking processes and start with a clean slate. I re-joined my church membership at Unity Gospel House of Prayer. It was time for me to clean my house, it felt wicked. I received blessed oil from my pastor and walked through my house anointing every window and door; every bedpost, every entrance with the oil and I prayed. I felt different. Chills ran through my body as I touched handrails and hallways throughout the house.

"God, I ask you to not allow any person into this house that doesn't belong here. I recognize you as my God, I am your daughter, you live here, and this is your dwelling place, in my heart and in my home. Rebuke the enemy from trying to enter this now sacred place." My prayer was sealed and heard in heaven. When I prayed, I believed it in my heart and I knew God heard me. I gave away the bed that I had been betrayed in and purchased a white heavenly looking bedroom set. I was broken, but I was at peace. Knowing God was with me, I couldn't feel the pain like I would have otherwise. Besides, I didn't have time to feel pain, my mother was sick and I had to focus on her.

I was now in a new relationship with the Lord, it was giving and uplifting. Those close to me would search me for pain in my eyes, they couldn't understand why I had no tears. Some chalked it up to me being a strong woman; it was just the opposite. I was weak, but in Christ, that is what made me strong. I knew that without the Lord, I would just go back or find someone else to be in a relationship with. I needed to stop the insanity and I knew that could only be done with the Lord's help. I wanted to be better for my only daughter at the time. She needed me to show her how to be a woman, not a mess.

I got pregnant with her between marriages. Once I got free from my first husband, I set out to do all of the things I thought I had missed out on. I became attracted to bad boys, they were so different from my first husband, the church musician. When I saw this particular guy in the club, I couldn't take my eyes off of him. He wreaked bad boy, he was exciting. For many weeks we only stared at each other across the club dance floor. He finally said something to me and from that moment on it was the craziest, wildest and most chaotic time in my life. I was on a roller coaster ride and what I thought was the most thrilling time of my life.

I knew he was a bad boy, but he took the term to a whole different level from what I thought. He had other women and they were just as bad as he was. I had no clue what I was getting myself into. I was jumped, chased, and attacked so many times it became my normal. My life was going nowhere fast. When I finally decided I had to leave him alone, before something really bad happened to me, I found out I was pregnant. Shortly after I told him I was having a baby, I received a call that he had been shot. Someone put a gun to his head and pulled the trigger, but the gun backfired. He ran, but still got a bullet in the shoulder. That was the first time we had a serious conversation. He knew God had spared his life and I knew it too, but it was still over for us. God didn't spare his life for me, He had other plans for him. To this day, he is an assistant pastor at a church in Milwaukee that my current church sometimes visits. It's weird seeing him there for both our daughter and me; he doesn't speak, he just stares.

As I stood with oil in hand, whimpering and panting from the spiritual cleansing of my house, thoughts of my past replayed through my mind. I couldn't blame anyone but myself. I had listened to the voices of others and even the voice of my flesh. I had never even considered seeking God and trying to understand if I was acting according to His will. "Forgive me Lord, I vow to never enter into another relationship unless you tell me to yourself!" I made up my mind to never be abused and mistreated again, and as long as I was with God, He wouldn't allow it. I knew He would be the man to protect me, love me and encourage me. He would keep the wrong people out of my life and hide me under His wing. I needed saving; the kind that God can give. So the oil was spread throughout the house and I felt safe in His arms. I didn't know what God had in store for me, but as long as I had Him in my life, I didn't even try to figure it out.

One day, as I was resting on my aunt's couch, the doorbell rang; it was Wayne. He saw my car in front of my aunt's house and decided to stop in to say hello. Really, he is still showing up unannounced! But this time, my life had already been changed for the better and besides, I was done with men. We chatted a little and I'm sure he could feel the cold vibe coming from me, so he left. "You know he's getting a divorce", my aunt rang out. Turns out, he had been visiting my aunt regularly and she knew all the details of his life and even shared some my life details with him. "I told him you were getting a divorce too", she added. I felt betrayed by her, but my curiosity had been peaked. It didn't matter anyway, I was serious about the vow I made to the Lord.

Suddenly, my mom passed away, (I'll talk about this in a later chapter); I was devastated. My life had been forever changed, and when Wayne heard about it he was there for me every step of the way, as a friend. I told Wayne of the vow I had made, and he understood it completely. He reassured me that we wouldn't get involved again unless the Lord himself showed us both. We were both receiving the same teaching at church. Wayne had gone through a rough marriage and divorce and didn't want to marry again unless it was real; we were in agreement. So we kept our relationship strictly platonic and we encouraged each other to be at every church service.

It was fun having him as a Christian friend. We began talking on the phone more and talking a lot about God. I had never experienced this before, it was incredible. My feelings were growing for him and in a different way. I had known him when I was a full-blown sinner, but to see him through God's eyes was truly refreshing. One day I called and invited him to dinner and he accepted. Right away, I recalled my sincere prayer asking God to block any person from entering my home that didn't belong there. God was making sure that everyone who entered belonged. It was incredible to see God protecting me. I now realized this was a defining moment in our relationship. Either Wayne was in or he was out; it wasn't up to me, it was up to God. I prayed, "God, if Wayne gives an excuse of why he can't show up for dinner, I will know that you blocked it and I will accept it and stop talking to him". I was serious, my vow to God was important and I had to stand on it no matter how bad it hurt. God had become the most important man in my life.

I was anxious about preparing dinner and hoping the phone wouldn't ring. I didn't want to lose Wayne again. This was the moment of truth, I was starting to prepare myself for the worse. I had to be strong. Rain was pouring outside, I worried he would use it as an excuse not to show up for dinner. The enemy made me feel like I was being ridiculous putting such trust in God. "Are you really going to let Wayne go if he doesn't feel like coming out in the rain?" the voice said to me. "What if he's tired or had a bad day at work? Are you really just going to stop being his friend because of your stupid vow to God?" the voice taunted.

"Shut Up!" I screamed, I'm sticking to my vow and that's that. The voice went away and it couldn't make me second guess what I told God. The doorbell rang. A feeling of relief came over me. I opened the door to a drenched and very visibly exhausted man. I was so giddy, he couldn't help but notice the big cheese smile on my face. When his foot crossed over the door threshold, I almost burst out in laughter. God allowed him to come in.

Wayne said, "I almost didn't show up the weather was so bad." My heart dropped, but I let him continue. "I pulled into the garage at home and was about to park and call you to tell you I wasn't coming, but something wouldn't let me. So, I pulled back out of the garage and here I am," he said. I thought I was going to pass out. That "Something" was at work again and it made sure Wayne showed up. Wayne was supposed to be here. We were married the following year and have been growing stronger in the Lord together with our family, for more than 15 years.

> *"Love is patient and kind. Love is not jealous or boastful or proud or rude. It does not demand its own way. It is not irritable, and it keeps no record of being*

wronged. It does not rejoice about injustice but rejoices whenever the truth wins out. Love never gives up, never loses faith, is always hopeful, and endures through every circumstance." I Corinthians 13:4-7 NLT

Too many times I have experienced the opposite of this description of love, I experienced bad love. Bad love is quarrelsome and cruel. Bad love is hateful and rude. Bad love is controlling, abusive, deceitful, and worst of all painful. Bad love has no winners, only losers. Bad love is hopeless, lonely and defeating through every circumstance. Bad love has a voice that is deafening, it screams insecurity and low self-esteem into a soul. It is by far the most effective tool of the enemy. Too often, bad love starts out resembling real love, but in time, it has to reveal itself. Bad love is able to conceal itself in the initial stages because it offers to fill a void that we as humans need to be filled. Love is essential to humans, we were meant to love and be loved.

The enemy knows that if true love is withheld from a human being, they will try to replace it with lust, food, a job, or just about anything to fill the void, but nothing else will ever work. Humans have been encountering Bad love for thousands of years. Look at this exchange between Jesus and the Samaritan woman: "Go and get your husband," Jesus told her. "I don't have a husband," the woman replied. Jesus said, "You're right! You don't have a husband— for you have had five husbands, and you aren't even married to the man you're living with now. You certainly spoke the truth!" *(St John 4:16-18 NLT)* Wow! Jesus told her all about herself. While reading this story in the Bible, I realized I use to be the "woman at the well", looking for love in men, my search always turned up fruitless. It wasn't until I met Jesus on my own well and He told me all about myself that I understood He was the man I needed in my life.

I had no idea how to love a man. I had never been shown. Love had never been physically demonstrated before me; I was not able to recognize it. My earthly father had never shown love to my mother, or me for that fact. I needed the love that Jesus had to offer. I had to go back to the love drawing board and get my fundamental understanding of true love corrected. I needed to love the Lord my God with all of my heart, all of my soul, all of my mind, and all of my strength (Mark 12:30), before I could properly love romantically. My delight was supposed to be in the Lord, not in man. I had allowed men to draw me away from the church, away from Jesus. I was so focused on being in a romantic relationship, that I left my one true everlasting love for temporary love. I had become more interested in the activities that pleased the man in my life, more than spiritual activities. I was craving a human relationship more than a relationship with Christ. I had fallen into fellowship with those who did not have a spiritual life. I realized that I had exhibited all of the signs of leaving my first love – God. Look at what Jesus told the church of Ephesus in Revelation 2:4-5 KJV:

4 Nevertheless I have somewhat against thee, because thou hast left thy first love. 5 Remember therefore from whence thou art fallen, and repent, and do the first works; or else I will come unto thee quickly, and will remove thy candlestick out of his place, except thou repent.

Here is another three-step process that Jesus is giving to help one rekindle the love for him. Remember – think back to when you were first saved and experienced the love of Christ. Remember the peace, security, freedom, and newness in Christ that made you feel love like you had never experienced before. Recall how God forgave you and gave you a fresh start; old things are passed away, behold all things have become new. Repent – change your mind towards things that have taken your attention away from your first love. Ask God for forgiveness and make a vow to never allow anything to separate you from the love of God. Renew your commitment to God. Do the First Works – It is time to get your priorities back in order. Start back doing those things that you did when you first fell in love with Christ. Praying, fasting, worshipping, praising, attending regular church services, fellowshipping with other believers, and studying the Word of God. Get back to working on your relationship with Christ, this is the most important relationship you will ever have.

It is very dangerous for a believer to leave their first love. But I am so glad that Jesus never leaves us stranded. We may leave Him, but He never leaves us. Jesus is our first love; He is the lover of our soul.

Oh, how I love Jesus
Oh, how I love Jesus
Oh, how I love Jesus
Because He first loved me

> *But God showed his great love for us by sending Christ to die for us while we were still sinners.*
> *Romans 5:8 NLT*

PRAYER

Most gracious heavenly Father, I love you. I commit to loving you with all of my heart, all of my mind, all of my soul, and all of my strength. Please forgive me for leaving you, my first true love. I have repented of putting human relationships before you. I have changed my ways of allowing worldly pleasures to come between the love that you and I share. Never again will I allow anything to separate me from your love. You showed your great love towards me when you sent your son to die for me while I was still a sinner. You loved me when I did not even love myself. I will always remember how I felt when I first fell in love with you. I will recall to my mind the peace, security, and freedom that your love gives me. Your love revives me and causes me to flourish. I would not know how to love, if I did not know you. You are love, and to know you is to know love. Your love will always be a priority for me. I love you, because you first loved me. In Jesus name. Amen!

CHAPTER FIVE

DEAF BY REJECTION

Psalm 94:14 NLT The LORD will not reject his people; he will not abandon his special possession.

I met rejection around the age of five in a courtroom full of adults. As I held my mother's hand tightly, I quickly learned she was the only adult in the room with my best interest in mind. I could not understand why my father was not standing next to my mother and me. I also could not understand why he was acting like we were strangers to him. "Mama, why didn't daddy say hi to me?" I could tell my mother was very upset. I got so angry, I did not know what was going on, but I knew enough to understand that my mother was being hurt.

I took off running towards my father and when I got close enough, I kicked him as hard as I could. "Daddy, why are you acting like you don't know me?" Everyone burst into laughter, but not my mother. I was not able to understand all that was being said between the adults. There was some shouting, some tears, and a lot of confusion on my part. When it was time for us to leave, my father and the other men (his team of lawyers) he was with walked by my mom and I like we did not exist. I could feel my mother's pulse in her hand as I held it tightly. We stood there as they walked by, one of the men told my dad, "Let us know when you're ready to get your daughter back", and they laughed.

My mother later explained to me that my dad denied that he was my father. I could not understand what I did to make him not want me anymore and say that I was not his daughter. *Even if my father and mother abandon me, the LORD will hold me close.* (Psalm 27:10 NLT) I had been abandoned. He refused to give me his name. He refused to teach me about boys. He refused to provide for me financially. He refused to protect me. This was the first of many encounters with rejection that I would endure throughout my life.

Whether personal or professional, you will get to hear the deafening sound of rejection, if you have not already. Satan has always used the voice of rejection as one of his vices. Rejection makes us feel ostracized, unwanted, and unloved. Rejection has its loudest voice when it comes from someone that you would never expect it from like a parent, spouse, close friend, or family member. Even Jesus experienced rejection from his own people. John 1:10 NLT *He came into the very world he created, but the world didn't recognize him. 11 He came to his own people, and even they rejected him.*

See, rejection did not even take a day off for our Lord and Savior Jesus Christ. The definition of reject, according to Merriam-Webster, is **to refuse to accept, consider, submit to, take for some purpose, or use.** [4] In my earliest experience with rejection as a child, my father was refusing to accept or consider me as his daughter. As I got older I asked him why he rejected me. His answer was, "I couldn't let my family find out that I had a black child, or I would lose my inheritance." The only problem I had with this, is that by the time I got this explanation from him, he had 2 more black children that he did not reject. Long story short, he was right, and ultimately disinherited for having black children. His disinheritance did not give me any peace however. Out of all of his children, it is only my birth certificate that says "Unknown" where the father's name is supposed to go.

For years I suffered from the rejection of my father. I literally chased him around town driving to different bars he hung out at to spend time with him, hoping to feel some kind of acceptance. My baby sister would get so annoyed with me for doing this. She was a lot stronger than me when it came to ignoring his unsympathetic fatherly ways. Even though his name was on her birth certificate, he treated us both the same. But for me it was worse, I acted out. I tried to find acceptance in men. I was determined to be accepted by a male figure. Well, from reading the previous chapter, you know that did not always work out so well for me.

I had been rejected so many times, that I began to expect it from people. I decided I would beat people to the punch and exclude myself from parties, trips, or even some family gatherings. There are some places you cannot exclude yourself from like the workplace, and then you run into rejection again.

I had been on my job for almost 3 years and it was time for me to make a move to a better paying position within the company. I posted for what I thought was a perfect position. I met all of the qualifications, experience needed, and educational requirements. My first interview went great, I was sure I had this job in the bag. My second interview was with the manager of the role I was applying for. During the interview, I noticed a lot of pauses from the manager, but I made sure to stay positive and focus on answering all questions accurately with well-thought-out responses. I felt good about the interview and was excited about the outcome. A week went by and I heard nothing. I called the manager and never got a return call. I finally called the recruiter that I had the first interview with and was transferred. "Kara, I'm going to transfer you to one of our human resource representatives so you can get more information."

This was weird, I have been through this process before and never had this happen. "Kara, we have been working with the manager on this position trying to find the best fit. So far you are the only applicant, which is really strange. We are waiting for more applicants to apply", the HR rep said. I understood that, so I waited another 2 weeks before I started my calls again. This time, I was asked to meet with a human resource specialist and the company's diversity specialist. "Kara you are still the only applicant for this job. We have not received one other internal or external applicant". I said, "That's great, so what's the problem. I know that I'm qualified for the position."

Finally, the diversity specialist says, "The manager of the position feels like you don't speak well and does not want to give you the job since you would be interacting with clients". My mouth dropped. I sat speechless thinking back over the interview with the manager.

"How can she say something like this?" I asked.

"We were hoping to get a better sense of why she would make such a statement, which is why we are meeting with you in person today", the diversity specialist said.

"So, you are meeting with me to see if I speak well?" I asked. Even they heard how ridiculous that sounded. "So, what do you think? Do I speak well to you?" I whipped. "It wasn't anything I said to her, it was how I look to her", I stated. I realized that the manager had to look my picture up in the company profile. They both knew I was right. I ended up getting the job, and the manager had to go through diversity training. She made sure I was miserable. This was by far the most stressful job I ever had. I had to document everything and make sure I was on point at all times.

What the devil meant for my downfall, turned out for my good. I did not see it then, but the rejection I endured made me stronger. My father's rejection made me self-reliant. My workplace rejection built a strong work ethic in me. Rejection made me want to be a better person, maybe not for the right reasons initially, but everything worked out for me in the end.

I take no credit for overcoming the rejection I faced. So many times the devil spoke rejection in my ears and I felt defeated. As I began to peel back the deafening voice of rejection, I could see God's hand at work in my life. I realized I was chosen to go through these trials to mold me into the woman I am today. There was a purpose in my rejection. While I was being rejected by people, I was being accepted by God. God did not accept me because I was perfect, or because I had something to offer Him; He accepted me because He loves me genuinely. For years, I allowed the rejection from others to define me. My identity was based on how others treated me and the closer they were to me, the deeper the hurt. But I have learned that Christ holds my true identity. Only what God says about me is true, because everything that God says is true.

Proverbs 30:5 NLT *Every word of God proves true. He is a shield to all who come to him for protection.*

Here is my identity in Christ:

I am the righteousness of Christ through faith

Because of God's great love for me, I'm adopted into His family

I am made joint heirs with Christ

I am blessed with spiritual blessings in Christ

I am chosen, a royal priesthood, a holy nation, God's special possession

I am forgiven

I am loved

I am the head and not the tail

I am above and not beneath

I am more than a conqueror

I am an overcomer

God's Holy Spirit has the full knowledge of who you are and is constantly leading and guiding us into the truth of who we are and what we are called to do for God. I believe what God says about me!

PRAYER

Heavenly Father, I thank you for accepting me. While those close to me, who I thought should take care of, rejected me, you were waiting with your arms open wide to receive me. All of the times I felt minimized and ostracized, you were working a great plan to show me how much I mean to you. Forgive me Lord for allowing the enemy to tell me who I was. Forgive me Lord for listening to the voices of hateful men and women who wanted my downfall to having a say in what I thought about myself. I will show love to those who have rejected me. I will not take revenge on those who have tried to exclude me. I know that one day, in your righteous judgment, you will right all wrongs. You will defend me and stand up for. With you on my side, who can come against me? You are my refuge and my shield, my trust is in you. I will always believe your words over any other word. Your Word is true. You know who I am, because I was created by you, for you. Thank you Lord for accepting me. I love you, In Jesus name. Amen.

CHAPTER SIX

DEAF BY ABUSING GRACE

Romans 6:1-2 NLT Well then, should we keep on sinning so that God can show us more and more of his wonderful grace? Of course not! Since we have died to sin, how can we continue to live in it?

"Amazing Grace, how sweet the sound, that saved a wretch like me. I once was lost but now I'm found, was blind but now I see."

I used to hear this song in church all the time as a child. This song crossed boundaries as it expressed the gratitude thousands of saints felt for the loving grace that God had extended towards them. This hymn was sung by different nationalities and by people from all sorts of backgrounds. It even poured off the lips of slaves who could identify God's grace even through their horrific circumstances. Amazing Grace became the spiritual anthem for thousands of churches across the country and the lyrics resonated within hearts. Ironically, this song was written by a man who was once a slave trader, John Newton.

> *"There he traveled from slave factory to slave factory, buying slaves and storing them in his ship, just like always, He sailed for the New World and studied his Bible as two hundred slaves were packed into shelving in the hold beneath him." (Jeremiah, 66)* [2]

God used a 10-year slave dealer to touch the lives of hundreds of thousands with the lyrics of "Amazing Grace". According to David Jeremiah, Newton wouldn't write "Amazing Grace" until twenty-five years after his conversion.

John traded slaves until one day he had his own encounter with Grace on a ship that changed his life forever. It took some time for John to realize that slavery was wrong as most believers during this time did not think it was. As the Holy Spirit speaks to John, he comes to understand how sinful slavery is:

> *Yet the committed believer begins to hear the voice of the Holy Spirit more clearly as time goes by. He begins to see the world as the Father sees it and to think with the mind of Christ. John Newton experienced a dawning horror about the true evil of his former vocation. (Jeremiah, 66)* [2]

From the heart of an ex-slave trader turned servant of God came the words to the song "Amazing Grace". I believe the reason this song reached and touched so many is because of the desperation it was written out of. I can understand how this man must have felt being changed from a most appalling human being, a wretch, to a change agent for Christ. His story is magnificent, but in many ways similar to thousands of others that God has reached way down to lift them out of darkness with His amazing grace.

My favorite Apostle from the Bible for example, Apostle Paul. Paul, like me, admitted openly that he was the greatest sinner of all. *(1 Timothy 1:15)* Before Paul had his own encounter with Grace, he was known as Saul of Tarsus who persecuted and pursued Christians. He chased them down, beat and condemned them. After he witnessed the cruel stoning death of Deacon Stephen, Saul's lust for Christian persecution was relentless. *(Book of Acts)*

One day as he was on a bloodthirsty Christian mission, Grace met him on a road to Damascus. His Grace encounter was so significant, that it led him to become one of the greatest apostles of Jesus Christ and helped usher in the grace movement by offering this wonderful saving grace to gentiles – like you and me. I pointed out these miraculous examples of God's grace, to show you that grace can assist a rank sinner in becoming a significant mouthpiece and vessel for Jesus Christ. In fact, the very definition of grace, according to the Merriam-Webster Dictionary, is the **unmerited divine assistance given humans for their regeneration or sanctification.** [3] Grace is God assisting us with our restoration and separation from the world. God is always leaning towards us and bestowing his favor on us because He wants so badly to be near us.

I would be foolish to not add my name to the long list of those grace captured and assisted. It is this very same grace that is aiding my thoughts and hands to write this book right now. I too, was a wretch saved by Grace, I once was lost, but now am found, was once blind but now I see. I am a grateful recipient of God's amazing grace through Christ Jesus. However, I'll be the first to admit that I haven't always reciprocated this precious grace that I have received to others. For years I used God's grace as a cushiony pillow to lay my head upon for my own comfort. It took a while for me to realize that God didn't give me this wonderful grace to sit on and soak it all up for myself. I did not see it clearly at the time, but now when I look back, I distinctly see the vicious and dangerous cycle of taking advantage of God's grace. I can understand where Jonah was coming from when he was so frustrated with God for being so forgiving to a people who didn't deserve it.

Let's take a look at Jonah's angry rant to God in Jonah 4:2 NLT *"So he complained to the LORD about it: "Didn't I say before I left home that you would do this, LORD? That is why I ran away to Tarshish! I knew that you are a merciful and compassionate God, slow to get angry and filled with unfailing love. You are eager to turn back from destroying people."* Jonah didn't think it was fair that God would use him to help people who were so dry and undeserving of His grace. Like Jonah, I also understood that God is rich in mercy, but I used it to my advantage. Unlike Jonah, I could never be upset with God for His unfailing love; I'm forever grateful for it. The Bible warns us that there are two very specific ways that we can abuse the Grace of God: exploiting grace as a free pass to sin and trying to take credit for it because of good works. This ill-perspective of grace can do much damage to the spiritual ear.

While Paul was teaching grace and establishing churches throughout the land, false teachers were coming in behind him and teaching a false grace doctrine. *"I know that false teachers, like vicious wolves, will come in among you after I leave, not sparing the flock. Even some men from your own group will rise up and distort the truth in order to draw a following." (Acts 20:29-30 NLT)* These false teachers, or wolves, distorted the gospel and taught that grace would cover up their sins so they could continue living immoral lives. Basically, these false doctrines instilled that it was acceptable to sin because believers are saved by God's amazing grace of a surety.

Unsurprisingly, this false teaching is still being taught today. People nowadays, love a good grace message, believing that the marvelous grace of Jesus Christ gives them a free pass to sin. They get cozy in their church pew and soak up the grace message that lulls them into a state of sin unconsciousness and a green light to walk out the doors unchanged. The false grace message delivers you from the guilt of sin, causing you to not have an awareness of sin at all; everything becomes acceptable. I fell victim to this voice that caused me to not be conscious of my sin while claiming to be saved.

I felt like I was missing out on life if I wasn't partying or doing whatever I wanted to do to please my flesh. "I'll just ask for forgiveness," I would often say. (Those words haunt me now). I would spend most of my week living as sinful as I pleased, and then get up early Sunday morning and run to church. I was a choir member and would often belt out a song "I am His Child" head banging from drinking the night before. I had no shame, I was a believer and certain grace would come through for me. No one could tell I was offering a half-hearted ministry hiding behind a false sense of grace that enabled me to have one foot in the church and the other in the club. At least I was going to church and singing in the choir, that had to count for something with God or so I thought.

I was abusing grace and taking God for granted without even realizing it. I was told that I was just a sinner saved by God's grace. While that's true, the enemy, with the help of my flesh, totally twisted the message and I applied it in a way that made me feel so powerless against sin, that instead of fighting against, I settled in it. "Oh well, I'm only human, born in sin and shaped in iniquity – this isn't my fault, it is Eve's fault." I was living life on a free pass of cunning theology. A war was raging within and I was losing. I had a serious case of the "I Can't Help Its" and continued tapping God for His grace. I was addicted to a false grace that deafened my inner ear from the heavenly voice that struggled to get an audience with me. I thought if I just went to church and fulfilled my religious obligations, I would be fine. I had never heard I was supposed to live a life well pleasing to God, so I lived a life pleasing to me and expected God's grace and his mercy to continue following me all the days of my life – Wrong!

Just like I was once foolish by abusing grace, thousands still remain abusers today. Look at this question Paul posed in Romans 6:1-2 NLT: *Well then, should we keep on sinning so that God can show us more and more of his wonderful grace? 2 Of course not! Since we have died to sin, how can we continue to live in it?* Do you really think you are above abusing God's grace? I hope that you are, but let's see. Is there someone that you haven't forgiven? Are you holding a grudge against someone? Are you seeking revenge on someone? Are you holding bitterness, resentment, or anger in your heart against someone? Has someone reached out to make peace with you and you refuse? If you answered yes to any of these or you have similar hidden unresolved issues, and you claim to have accepted Jesus, you are guilty of abusing grace. Hebrews 12:14-15 NIV *Make every effort to live in peace with everyone and to be holy; without holiness no one will see the Lord. See to it that no one falls short of the grace of God and that no bitter root grows up to cause trouble and defile many.* We can actually fall short of the grace of God by allowing bitterness to defile us. The enemy whispers in our ears that it is not a big deal, and that you can just sweep this under the rug like it never happened, and God will forgive you.

Before you know it, your rug has all kinds of lumps in it from hiding the indiscretions that can't be seen with human eyes. Consider this scripture: *Catch all the foxes, those little foxes, before they ruin the vineyard of love, for the grapevines are blossoming! (Song of Solomon 2:15 NLT)* It's the little foxes that spoil the vine. The little foxes are great in number: small compromises here and there, unseen disobedience to God's voice, overlooked pleasing of the flesh, little white lies, gossiping, backbiting, undercover hating, envious of others, and the list goes on. But Jesus tells us not to even bring a gift to the altar if we know that a brother or sister has something against you, but go reconcile first. *(Matthew 5:23-24)*

Jesus is telling us here that we can't cover up our bad relationships or sweep issues under the rug by performing a religious duty. It's more important to Jesus that we extend grace to each other than put money in an offering basket hoping to feel better about our trespass. Believers who harbor ill feelings towards one another is a growing disease that is setting up infections in our spiritual ears. This disease causes some to engage in deliberate and habitual sin, proving that they don't have the spirit of Christ at all. Let's review Matthew 22, to see what happens to a person who has become accustomed to abusing God's Grace and trying to conceal it in plain sight:

> *Jesus also told them other parables. He said, 2 "The Kingdom of Heaven can be illustrated by the story of a king who prepared a great wedding feast for his son. 3 When the banquet was ready, he sent his servants to notify those who were invited. But they all refused to come! 4 "So he sent other servants to tell them, 'The feast has been prepared. The bulls and fattened cattle have been killed, and everything is ready. Come to the banquet!' 5 But the guests he had invited ignored them and went their own way, one to his farm, another to his business. 6 Others seized his messengers and insulted them and killed them. 7 "The king was furious, and he sent out his army to destroy the murderers and burn their town. 8 And he said to his servants, 'The wedding feast is ready, and the guests I invited aren't worthy of the honor. 9 Now go out to the street corners and invite everyone you see.' 10 So the servants brought in everyone they could find, good and bad alike, and the banquet hall was filled with guests. 11 "But when the king came in to meet the guests, he noticed a man who wasn't wearing the proper clothes for a wedding. 12 'Friend,' he asked, 'how is it that you are here without wedding clothes?' But the man had no reply. 13 Then the king said to his aides, 'Bind his hands and feet and throw him into the outer darkness, where there will be weeping and gnashing of teeth.' 14 "For many are called, but few are chosen."*

As I read this parable of Jesus, I immediately saw the grace of God. Jesus was explaining how grace works in figurative storytelling. The King was throwing a huge wedding celebration for his Son. The guest list was all drawn up, but everyone on the initial invite refused to come. The King was determined to not have an empty banquet hall, so the invitation went out to anyone who would accept. I'm sure the hall was filled with ones that didn't really deserve to be there, but they accepted the invitation, got dressed in their best apparel, and showed up for the party. Now here comes the scary part. The King comes in to greet His guests and He notices one particular man is not properly dressed for the party and the King had him thrown out of the party and into darkness.

What made this man so noticeably different to the King? Everyone else had gotten dressed properly to honor and celebrate the Son, but this man had no such intentions. Clearly, this underdressed man wanted all of the great tasting food and fun, but was not interested at all in the King or His son, only what they had to offer. This man abused the King's kindness and graciousness and was only seeking to benefit himself. As I ponder on this parable more, this man was most likely sewing discord among the other guests. Or maybe even igniting heresy against the King and his Son; hence, starting a rebellion among the invitees.

Can you imagine this underdressed man complaining about the menu, the decorations, and the guest list? He most likely wanted all of the attention for himself, which is why he was dressed differently than everyone else who came to celebrate the King's son. While the other guests took the invitation seriously and put away their old clothes and dressed in righteous apparel, this man was wearing a disguise. The disguise was so good, it got him on the invite list and into the banquet hall. He may have fooled many in his costume, but the King saw right through it and had him thrown out of the party and into darkness.

When I read this chapter, I realize many can easily be like the underdressed man. The giant of abusing grace is so subtle, we gloss right over it and keep on giving our gifts at the altar, completing our religious duties, and pretending like there is nothing wrong. It is time to expose this sin we have grown so accustomed to that will stop us from entering those pearly gates. We must understand that God's grace is in the details, assisting us in every area of our lives, but we must pay attention to it and accept the help. We can't afford to dress in play clothes pretending to be righteous. We must allow God's Grace to strip off the old sinful clothes and assist in putting on Christ. *Instead, clothe yourself with the presence of the Lord Jesus Christ. And don't let yourself think about ways to indulge your evil desires. (Romans 13:14 NLT)*

God's grace is still working in your life to help you not slip back into the bondage of sin. So, let's accept God's grace for the wonderful gift that it is and never take our Lord for granted.

2 Corinthians 6:1-3 NIV As God's co-workers we urge you not to receive God's grace in vain. 2 For he says, "In the time of my favor I heard you, and in the day of salvation I helped you." I tell you, now is the time of God's favor, now is the day of salvation.

PRAYER

Most gracious heavenly Father, I thank you for your Grace and your Mercy. You go above and beyond for me by extending your outstretched hand of Grace to me. Your favor has covered me even when I did not deserve it. I thank you for teaching me that I should never take your Grace for granted. I thank you for showing me that your Grace is a gift from you that I am not able to work for. You show your Grace to me, because it is who you are and I am forever in your gratitude. Help me Lord to show Grace to my brothers and sisters as we travel on this journey together. I desire to never take your Grace for granted, and allow your wonderful Grace to make all of the necessary changes in me so that I can be whole. I will allow your loving Grace to remove the layers of sin from my life and dress me in righteous clothing helping me to put on Christ. And to prove that you live in me, I will extend your wonderful Grace to someone else and not hold it all for myself. Amen!

CHAPTER SEVEN

DEAF BY DEATH

Ecclesiastes 7:1-2 NLT A good reputation is more valuable than costly perfume. And the day you die is better than the day you are born.
2Better to spend your time at funerals than at parties. After all, everyone dies—
so the living should take this to heart.

Death has a sound. It screams in your inner ear- grabbing your attention at the most inconvenient times. Its taunting voice is telling us that it is coming for us all, and there is absolutely nothing we can do about it. We cringe at the idea of it. As we lay restless in our beds, our throats sting from the pain of trying to hold back tears at the thought of loved ones falling into the hands of the fourth horseman – Death. *(Revelation 6:8)*

One night I witnessed it speak to my son Nigel. He was getting food from the refrigerator, when suddenly he broke into an uncontrollable sob. I begged him to tell me what was wrong, but he didn't want to speak it. Something had terrified him and it began to terrify me. Finally, he told me, out of nowhere, the thought of me dead had crushed his soul. He was not able to control the anguish that gripped his mind with no warning. I tried to comfort him, but I knew it was futile. Death had whispered in his ear and drove him to a dark place that he dreaded. I understood how he felt, death had spoken to me often. I would try to shut out this mortal voice with prayer and happy thoughts, but it always returned.

Death is so loud, that when it strikes, many believers convert into atheists. Countless lose faith in God and stop believing that He exists once death steps in and claims a loved one. Many believers question God, asking why won't He intervene and stop death in the very act. If you're looking for comfort from death, you may not want to go to the book of Ecclesiastes in the Bible; you'll only get a painstaking dose of reality.

> *"This, too, I carefully explored: Even though the actions of godly and wise people are in God's hands, no one knows whether God will show them favor. 2 The same destiny ultimately awaits everyone, whether righteous or wicked, good or bad, ceremonially clean or unclean, religious or irreligious. Good people receive the same treatment as sinners, and people who make promises to God are treated like people who don't. 3 It seems so wrong that everyone under the sun suffers the same fate. Already twisted by evil, people choose their own mad course, for they have no hope. There is nothing ahead but death anyway. 4 There is hope only*

for the living. As they say, "It's better to be a live dog than a dead lion!"" (Ecclesiastes 9:1-4 NLT)

The writer, however insensitive he may sound, is letting us know it doesn't matter who you are, believer or not, good or bad, we all share the same fate, we are all going to die. I'm not sure what made Solomon, the believed writer of this text, have such a gloomy outlook on life. He was known as the wisest king, had many riches and hundreds of wives. Clearly, he didn't like that we all have the same fate, he didn't think it was fair. We don't think it is fair either. Admit it! Children die young from terrible diseases. Stray bullets kill innocent people. Soldiers are gunned down fighting wars in foreign lands. Reckless or drunk drivers take hundreds of lives a year, and usually walk away unscathed. Our loved ones depart too soon leaving us with broken hearts.

Like Solomon, many feel that it is so wrong that everyone under the sun suffers the same fate. Why should a believer and a rank sinner suffer the same fate? I too, felt the same way at one point in life, but not any longer. I had to go on a death journey to understand that my perspective needed to change.

"God, what do you want from me"? I screamed as loud as I could in my living room, in hopes He would stop what He was doing and turn His attention to me. It seems senseless to me now. Who was I to stop God in His tracks to come and see about me; what had I offered to expect such Grace? I knew I hadn't lived my life according to His word, but I was desperate. I had to try. "If you save her, I'll give you my life. I'll serve you for real. I'll even change my church membership to one that will help me focus better, so that you'll know I'm serious. Please God, don't take my mother, I need her, my kids need her."

I opened the Bible and decided to read the first chapter I opened up to. This test worked once before when I needed to hear from God, I gave it another try. I was hoping to get a glaring response that would comfort me and tell me that anything I ask I would get if I believed. I was ready to believe. Instead, I got – nothing. He chose to be silent and leave me in anguish. I lay there crying, hopeless, and afraid. Trying to imagine my existence without that one person who remained consistent in my life – my mother. The pains stung in my chest and stomach. Death was coming, and I could feel it. God's silence spoke volumes and there was nothing I could do. I tried to continue my bribe with God. "My service, for her life here on earth with me". As I bargained, she lay in a coma, hospital-bound, and body swelled with fluid from congestive heart and kidney failures, unable to breathe on her own. "She deserves to live God, she's much better than I have been. She loves you and sings to you and prays to you, she talks about you all the time. I'll stop allowing distractions to come between us, if you will spare her life."

The silence rang so loud, my head was splitting from the pain. I wasn't convinced that God had accepted my deal, but I thought I better make good on my part, just in case. I changed my church membership and decided I would focus on learning the Word. I put myself on time out from singing in the choir and just sat and listened as a lay member. Two days later, my mother was out of the coma and back smiling again. I was elated, God heard me, I thought, he accepted my plea. She wasn't out of the woods and needed to start dialysis. She was so afraid of dialysis and did not want to go through with it. The doctor's pressed her, that without it she would die, so she finally accepted. Going to dialysis was scary, the catheter was placed in her neck initially and we were told it would be moved to her arm later. I usually dropped her off at dialysis on my lunch break and picked her up after work, but May 6, 2002 didn't go as scheduled.

I received a phone call before lunch that she was in the hospital and had had four heart attacks. I rushed to the hospital to see her laying there, unable to speak, looking at me for comfort. "It's gonna be ok Mama". That's all I had for the woman who always had comforting words for me. The doctors told us there was still a chance as they could perform emergency heart surgery. "God please help me, I thought we had an understanding. I have been making good on my part of the deal. Don't take her, please. Let the surgery work." As they rushed her to the operating room, she had another heart attack and the doctor came and told us she was gone. Was God playing a sick joke on me? Why get my hopes up, knowing He would allow me to be crushed. I slammed my fists on the table over and over again. I screamed to the top of my lungs. The doctor ran out of the room, closing the door behind him, leaving my family and me to our torment.

I looked around at my family as they sobbed quietly, but I was angry. "You didn't have enough stock with God to make the deal. Did you really think he would listen to you after a few weeks of you trying to live right? Looks like the jokes on you!" The voice laughed me to scorn, it tormented and ridiculed me. It was right, I was foolish to think I could bargain with God for my mother's life. For a short time, I thought I had held off death. I thought I would have her with me longer, but death came with mercilessness and without warning. The catheter in her neck, set up an infection that traveled to her heart causing multiple heart attacks. Death used the very thing that frightened her, dialysis, to place her on his horse and ride her away into eternity. Death didn't care how wonderful my mother was to me or how much I needed her. Death came for a woman with a heart of gold, and left me here to suffer through life, without her.

I felt doomed, May 6, 2002 changed my life forever. To add insult to injury, my little sister and I buried her the day before Mother's day. I found myself laughing at the irony. My heart was swollen with despair, I thought it might explode. The effects of this particular death were so loud, I couldn't begin the healing process; I wasn't able to mourn. Voices tortured me, especially at night. "You should have taken her to the hospital the night before", the voice scolded. "What kind of daughter are you? You should have tried to live your life for God a long time ago," it continued.

I walked around for weeks after the funeral angry with people for moving on with their lives. "Nobody really cares," the voice chided. I knew the voice was trying to isolate me so it could work on drawing me closer to it again. I had been through enough to not fall for that again, I refused. I needed to make sense of it all, it didn't seem fair to me. I continued going to church seeking answers from God. I began going to Bible study and prayer services during the week, I was on a mission. I needed to understand how to make it in this world without my mother and I needed God to explain this tragedy to me. One Tuesday night during prayer service, the Apostle appealed to the congregation: "As I call out what you are dealing with in your life, come forward to be anointed with oil and receive the breath of life". I waited anxiously, maybe this is my moment, but he never called out what I was going through. Finally, I was the only one left still standing in the whole sanctuary, waiting for help. The Apostle walked over to me and asked, "What are you going through?"

"My heart is broken," was all I could say before bursting into tears. It was literally breaking, I thought

I might have a heart attack just like my mom. He stood firm in front of me with a look that sent shivers down my spine. He walked me through asking for forgiveness and confessing Christ as my personal savior. He then anointed me with oil, prayed for me and blew the breath of life into my mouth. I didn't understand what was happening to me, my knees buckled, and I plummeted to the floor. I felt a calming sensation all over my body and all I could do was give God thanks. Somehow, at that moment, I knew I would be alright. I confessed right into my salvation and received the gift of deliverance. God forgave me for acting out of desperation. He comforted me, He didn't want to see me hurting.

I drew near to Him and He drew near to me. "To prove that God is going to heal your heart, your mother is going to come to you in a dream", the Apostle proclaimed. When he spoke, I believed it. My mustard seed sized faith was beginning to sprout. Months went by and I realized that I hadn't cried in a while over the loss of my mother. "God, I thank you for comforting me. You healed my broken heart and filled me with a strength I never had. I thank you for giving her to me, for the time that I had with her and all she imparted to me. I know you loved her too, even more than I did. If it is alright with you Father, please let me cry for her right now," I prayed.

Out of nowhere, rivers of tears ran down my face and I fell to the floor. I was mourning, finally, the right way. My anger was gone and I was lamenting because the world had lost some of its light when my mother left. My hands lifted and praise began to ring from my lips. I went from wailing to praising, God was with me and He helped me mourn the right way – by praising Him. Exhausted from crying and praising, I fell asleep still fully clothed. Suddenly, the room was filled with brightness, but I couldn't see windows or lights. I heard a rhythmic beeping noise and turned to see where it was coming from. My mother was lying in a hospital bed, dressed in all white, glowing. The beeping sound was coming from the heart monitor she was hooked up to. I stood there looking at how beautiful she was, smiling and so peaceful. Out of nowhere, the monitor began slowing down, so I ran and jumped on the bed with her and started CPR. I was breathless and pumping her chest as hard as I could. The whole time she just laid there smiling, her body was still even though I was thrusting into her chest.

"Mama, hold on, I'm gonna help you!" I made sure my hands were positioned in the right place, just like I had learned in health class. I drove, hand over hand, into her chest harder and with more determination, but she never moved; she just lay there calm and smiling at me.

She finally broke the silence, "Kara, if you don't stop, you're going to hurt me." Her calm voice, shook me out of my frenzy. Still smiling so peacefully, "Kara, I'm fine," she revealed to me.

"You are, mama?" I asked. The beeping was slowing steadily. I didn't want to stop the chest compressions, but knew I had to.

"Yes, I'm fine baby," she whispered. I never stopped looking at her, I had never seen her look so beautiful before. I slowly removed my hands from her chest. The monitor beeped slower and slower until it gave up a long steady sigh, giving me proof that I had stopped. She was still smiling while the heart monitor released its final song. The brightness was gone and I was frantically looking around the room. My arms were weak and shaking; it took a few seconds for me to realize that I had been dreaming. Somehow, I could still hear the continuous and steady beep of the heart monitor from my dream. How can this be? I stood in the middle of the room looking around and realized, the recurrent sound was coming from my TV indicating the station had stopped its programming for the night. The sound from my dream rang out in concert with the sound in my bedroom signifying that I had let go of my misery of being without her. My heart was healed and she visited me just like the Apostle had prophesied.

Solomon is right, the same destiny awaits everyone. One day, I will have to travel the same path as my sweet mother. Death comes for us all. But wait a minute, doesn't that make it fair? Isn't it actually fair that we all die? Death is not racist, it doesn't discriminate against the poor and it does not fall victim to sexism, classism, or ageism. It would not be fair if death could be bargained with. It would not be fair if death only came for people who made mistakes. It would not be fair if death only sought out those with disabilities. There is no respect of persons with Death, God will not allow death to differentiate between us. What is even fairer about death coming to us all, is that it is not a secret. Death screams at us to be prepared for it, but we do not want to listen. We encounter it daily, directly, or indirectly, one way or another; yet, when it comes we are traumatized and unsuspecting.

We fall out of love with God and tear up the world with our wrath because death caught us off guard. I would like to suggest, that it is not death that is unfair, nor God, but our own perspectives and ill-preparedness that make death unscrupulous and unethical in our eyes. Don't get me wrong, I know death comes with a pain that can leave you balled up in knots for days. What I am saying is that a healthy perspective of death can prevent you from ever balling up, going into a depression so deep that you must be medicated, blaming God, or turning away from God, wanting revenge, or being angry. If we are honest with ourselves, and realize that death can come for anyone at any time, even our loved ones, we can begin to cultivate a healthy viewpoint so that when it strikes we are not shaken to our core. I thought death was being cruel to my son Nigel when it spoke to him that night in the kitchen, but it was warning him that one day he is going to encounter a significant death, so he would be smart to prepare. Yes, that is right, prepare. We should prepare for a good death. I would like to offer some steps towards preparation for a good death.

ACCEPT CHRIST AS YOUR PERSONAL SAVIOR.

To Mary Magdalene's surprise, when she went to the tomb where Jesus was laid, it was empty. I'm not suggesting that you surrender to a dead savior, but a risen savior, the only one who conquered death. Jesus accepted the role of savior so graciously even though He had to experience a traumatic death as a human. He felt every strike, whip, kick, slap, nail and any other cruel act the Romans could imagine to do to him. With one purpose in mind, Jesus endured a torturous death, so that death would not have the final say over our lives. If you want to teach death a lesson, accept Jesus Christ. God always had a plan to conquer death and provide his children with a way of escaping its grip. Jesus broke the power of death and showed us the way to eternal life.

Look at what 2 Timothy 1:9-10 NLT says: *For God saved us and called us to live a holy life. He did this, not because we deserved it, but because that was his plan from before the beginning of time—to show us his Grace through Christ Jesus. 10 And now he has made all of this plain to us by the appearing of Christ Jesus, our Savior. He broke the power of death and illuminated the way to life and immortality through the Good News.* Jesus abolished death and offers everlasting life to all who believe in Him. *For God so loved the world, that he gave his only begotten Son, that whosoever believeth in him should not perish, but have everlasting life. (John 3:16)*

REPENT AND LIVE.

God takes no pleasure in the death of His children, it was never His intention for us to die. It is for this very reason that He sent us His Word in the form of the Bible and in his only begotten son Jesus, who is also called the Word of God. *(John 1:14)* His word is constantly telling us to repent and come out of sin. *For I take no pleasure in the death of anyone, declares the Sovereign LORD. Repent and live! (Ezekiel 18:32 NIV)*

Repent and live! Show everyone with the beautiful expression of baptism that you have turned from wickedness and now have a surrendered life in Christ. Go down in the liquid grave, dying to sin, and rise to a new life that will lead you into eternal bliss with God. Take joy in this new life, no longer slave to sin, and live it to the fullest because you earned it through your obedience. God wants us to live happy and prosperous lives here on earth without transgressing. Live out your righteous life now and get all that God has in store for you on this side of heaven.

GET YOUR HOUSE IN ORDER.

Get right church and let's go home! I used to love singing this song in church standing next to my mom.

I never understood what it meant exactly, but I do now. If there is anyone in this world that you need to ask forgiveness, do it now. Forgive the ones who have hurt you. If you've hurt someone or tried to teach someone tough love and you went too far, now is the time to apologize. If you are not on speaking terms with a family member or friend, even if you don't know why, reach out to them and reconcile. If you have not shown gratitude to those who have helped you along the way, call them and tell them thank you.

If you had an argument with someone, and you still think you are right, call a truce. Tell your children you are proud of them for small accomplishments. Throw a party and invite people who would not expect it. Send out text messages and share the love of Christ. Tell your friends and family just how much you love them and appreciate them. If you owe someone money, pay your debt. Tell that person who is special to you, why they are so special. Resist evil. Tame your tongue. Leave this world with clean hands and a pure heart.

PLAN AHEAD

Eating healthy foods and regular exercise have benefits, even the Bible says so in 1 Timothy 4:8. A healthy lifestyle may prevent you from getting certain diseases, but it won't stop a freak accident from occurring, so planning ahead is imperative. The cause of death and the timing of death scream louder than the knowledge that this is something we should all plan for. We cannot afford to walk around living our lives as if death cannot happen to us. Here are some ways we can plan ahead:

1. **Get Life Insurance.** Please don't allow your unpaid bills and funeral expenses to fall to your family to figure out. Out of all the ways we claim death to be unfair, this is by far the most unfair – leaving debt and funeral expenses behind. Your family can't properly grieve over the loss of you, if they are too busy trying to figure out how to bury you.

2. **Contact the Funeral Home and Cemetery** of your choice and make payments and arrangements now.

3. **Start Paying Your Debt Off Now.** Get rid of credit cards and other non-essential bills. Make sure that you are not behind on rent, mortgages, and car notes.

4. **Plan Your Own Funeral Service.** Take the stress away from your family by writing your own obituary. Detail out where you want to be buried, what funeral home should care for your remains, what outfit you will have on, who you want to pray, read scripture, and even sing. Plan the whole celebration. Take out all of the guesswork. Your family will appreciate you for it and there will be smiles

mixed with tears. They will be able to focus on the time they had with you and not fight over if there will be a repast or not. Even better, you get exactly what you wanted.
5. **Make a Will and Testament.** Write out exactly who you want any monies, property, clothes, etc. to go to. Be specific or there will be a family feud. Get your beneficiaries in place so that your assets go to exactly who you want them to go to. If you own a business, be specific on who it should go to.

Planning for a peaceful departure from this earth will help your loved ones deal with the loss of you; it is the responsible thing to do. You do not want to be the reason family members are not speaking to each other, you want to be the reason they got closer. You especially want to be the reason they got closer to Christ. Change your perception of death. Live your life to the fullest, showing the love of Jesus Christ to your neighbor like you love yourself and great will be your reward in heaven – but first you have to make sure you get there. Don't allow death to shatter your spiritual ear because of your perception of it. Take heart beloved, death does not have the final say. *And God shall wipe away all tears from their eyes; and there shall be no more death, neither sorrow, nor crying, neither shall there be any more pain: for the former things are passed away. (Revelation 21:4)*

PRAYER

Most gracious heavenly Father, I know death isn't what you intended for me. Acts 2:10 told me that you had good things planned for me from the very beginning. Please forgive me for losing faith in you because death took someone special from me. Please forgive me for shattering under the pressure of death and not holding it together and standing strong when it arrived for someone I love. I understand that we are all going to die because of sin, but I am so grateful that you did not allow death to have the final say over my life. I thank you Father for sending your only begotten son Jesus into this world, so that you could give us a way to escape the grip of death. Jesus, I thank you for the precious blood you shed on Calvary so that I might enjoy life eternally with you. Jesus, you endured a horrible death and then you rose and defeated it. Because you defeated death, and I am in you, death will no longer defeat me. I believe that everyone who believes in you will not die, but have everlasting life. I will no longer let my heart be troubled. If you could go away to prepare a place for me, I will prepare to move in. I accept your gift of eternal life through Jesus Christ. Amen!

CHAPTER EIGHT

DEAF BY UNGUARDED HEART

Proverbs 4:23 Keep thy heart with all diligence; for out of it are the issues of life.

"Follow your heart, and you will find happiness" is what the world tells us. The only problem with that is we are all born with a heart condition. If it is happiness you want, then following your heart is not the path you want to take. God has been trying to protect us from heart issues since the creation. He warned Adam and Eve about the Tree of knowledge of good and evil, that eating from it would cause heart issues that would surely lead to death. He is still warning us all today that the heart cannot be trusted. *Jeremiah 17:9 The heart is deceitful above all things, and desperately wicked: who can know it?*

Adam and Eve went against God's advice by following their hearts and brought sure death upon us all. Instead of receiving happiness and being like gods, they were kicked out of their beautiful home, separated from God's presence, endured guilt and shame, had to toil to grow food, suffered painful childbirths, experienced the loss of a son, and eventually died; all because they let the guard down from their hearts. That same serpent that deceived Eve in the Garden of Eden, is still working to deceive us all today. Eve developed a heart condition when Satan planted a seed of curiosity and played a word game of semantics called, "You won't surely die," that led to disobedience. The heart deceiving ball began rolling; Satan deceived Eve, Eve deceived Adam, and on and on it goes until this very day.

Jesus explained to his disciples that it is the condition of the heart that really defiles a person. For out of the heart proceed evil thoughts, murders, adulteries, fornications, thefts, false witness, blasphemies. *(Matthew 15:15-20)* Jesus is saying, we are defiled inside out, not outside in. I am not talking about our physical hearts that work to pump blood through our bodies, but rather our soulful hearts. We are living souls, with a spirit to connect with God, encased in a body made of earthly clay. The soul is very complex; it is the essence of who we are. It is how we think, act, and make decisions; it is what makes you, you. It is where the battle between good and evil is being fought. Right now, inside of your very being, is a raging war between righteousness and wickedness.

The righteous defenders are fighting with weapons of God's word, faith, peace, and love; while, the wicked destroyers fight with lies, depression, temptation, lust, strongholds, and doubt. Your soul now has to make free will choices to do what it believes is best. The choices our souls make can be influenced by people, experiences, backgrounds, traditions, habits, society, and voices we may come in contact with. I also like to call these "influencers" giants. We have grown so accustomed to these giants because we have endured them for most of our lives, they have become our norm and we usually don't even recognize them. It is this nonchalant attitude of what is happening around us and within us every day that is the number one cause of our soul's heart disease known as deception. The heart is the cage that is holding all of the evil impulses that come flying right out of our mouths and even though we try, we cannot hide it. *"But the words you speak come from the heart--that's what defiles you." (Matthew 15:18 NLT)*

My own heart had been deceived and for years I lived with its side effects: procrastination, doubt, fear, low self-esteem, poverty, fornication, lies, depression, and the list goes on. Life planted some bitter seeds in me that I did not stand a chance against. My soul had inherited a disease that had been passed down to me. My heart disorder told me that I was not good enough, I was not loved, and that most people really did not like me. I spent many years of my life trying to fit in by making sure I did not stand out too much. I was always fine with taking the back seat to others, as I did not feel I belonged anyway. The poverty I grew up in shouted that I would never have better and made me complacent about being poor. Wanting to feel the love of a man screamed so loudly, I had rushed into a marriage of abuse and adultery.

My heart issues were constantly multiplying. I was being molded by negative experiences of others whose hearts were even more congested with issues than mine. "Sorry baby, I can't let my family know I have a black child, they would disinherit me." "You're not that pretty, I've had girlfriends that look better than you." "I can't give you the job because you don't speak well." Sticks and stones may break my bones, but words will never hurt me. Not true! Not only do they hurt, but they come back and sting over and over again. Wall after wall went up, trying to protect myself from people and their heart issues that would come flying out of their mouths at me. Soon I became known as quiet, but it was really despondent, shy, but it was actually withdrawn.

When God called me into the ministry, there was no way I could accept; my heart wouldn't let me. "You don't want to use someone like me God, you are definitely not getting a good deal. It's not you God, it's me." My diseased heart convinced me that it was silly to think God would want to have anything to do with me. I quickly rattled off a list of horrible things I had done in the past to Him (as if He didn't know). I thought I had settled that issue with God and that since He had been reminded of my wretchedness, He would be satisfied and find someone else to fulfill this call, but He didn't give up that easy. One night, I was seeing my little sister, Terri, and her family out the door and I shouted out my usual saying, "I love you, good night, yawl are the salt of the earth."

Right away, a voice asked me, "Do you know what you are saying? Do you know what that means?" I stood in the doorway frozen with a smile on my face.

No one could even tell that I had stopped in my tracks to have an internal conversation with God right in the middle of saying goodnight to my family. "I guess I don't really know what that means God, will you help me"? An excitement came over me, I needed to close the door so that I could grab my Bible and my iPad. I began researching the scripture "You are the salt of the earth. But what good is salt if it has lost its flavor? Can you make it salty again? It will be thrown out and trampled underfoot as worthless. *(Matthew 5:13 NLT)* Before I knew it, I had pages of notes on what this scripture meant to me and various uses for salt. I absolutely love the way David Jeremiah explains why Christians are called the salt of the earth:

"Why do people come to Christ? It's because they are thirsty. Something is lacking in their lives; they are parched because everything else seems so dry and empty. It's not a coincidence that the Bible calls Christians the salt of the world.

My uncle had a farm, and I remember asking him one time why he had those big chucks of salt where the cattle could lick them. He said it was because they needed to get thirsty and hungry enough to eat nutritious food."

Basically, Pastor Jeremiah is saying that Christians are the chunks of salt walking the earth causing the thirsty appetite in sinners to want to eat on the Word of God.

I had never felt so engaged and thrilled about studying anything in my life. Hours went by and I didn't even realize it; I was so engulfed on understanding what the Spirit was telling me. Suddenly it dawned on me, I was communicating with God the Holy Spirit and He was actually teaching me. "Wait a minute God, why are you spending time with me like this? Are you saying this scripture is for me? Could I possibly be salt, the kind you are talking about?" I realized God wasn't giving up on calling me into the ministry; there was something He wanted from me and He was determined to get it. As I studied more about salt, I learned that it has many uses but the one that stuck out to me most is a preservative. Salt was also so precious in the time of Jesus walking the earth, that Roman soldiers were sometimes paid in salt and this is where the saying "worth his salt", was coined. Not only that, many people use salt to make food more flavorful.

The Holy Spirit was telling me that I'm worth what Jesus paid for me and that I'm precious and have something special to offer the world to help preserve it and make it more flavorful or pleasant. I felt like I had drifted to a heavenly realm; I was in a state of euphoria. God was with me and He cared enough about me to stop me at my front door to start a conversation with me about what I meant to him. Suddenly, I was jerked back to reality, my heart issues began yelling at me. "Are you serious, how can God think you are the salt of the earth? Who do you think you are?"

I had never felt so much confusion, I wanted to cry. I wanted so badly to believe what I had just experienced was true, but my heart reminded me that I was not worthy of such a wonderful calling. I decided to put God to test. "God, if you are calling me into the ministry, tell my pastor to tell me." There, that should do it. Once again, I thought I had settled this issue with God and it wouldn't come up again because I knew my pastor was not going to tell me I was called into the ministry. That Sunday, I sat in church eager to receive the word, the pastor had only said hello to me in passing so I was safe. As the pastor stood and began his opening sermon remarks, he said, today's subject is "Salt of the earth". My heart skipped a few beats and I began to perspire in my seat. "Did this just happen? Did he just say – salt"? I felt like somehow the pastor had eavesdropped on the discussion between the Holy Spirit and me or God had just responded to my request; it couldn't have been the latter, no way, no how. A symptom of my heart disease began yelling at me – doubt. "That was just a coincidence, you know God is not going to respond to you, He doesn't have time for your petty games."

This was now the third time I had settled this issue with God regarding my call; I'm sure by now He's growing tired of me. Several months went by and I didn't have another conversation with God, I was afraid to. One day, something felt weird in my right breast and as I examined myself, it was a huge lump. I quickly set up an appointment to have a mammogram; they got me in right away. I was terrified as the nurses and mammogram technicians looked at me suspiciously not saying anything, but I could see what they were thinking. "We found several lumps in your left and right breasts, we need you to come back tomorrow for an ultrasound." I was devastated and I needed one of those conversations with God. "God, are you punishing me? I know I didn't accept your call, but I really thought I was doing right by you. Please don't punish me. Am I like Jonah? Is this my whale experience? I had so many questions for God, but He remained silent. I had not told anyone what I was going through, I thought that would make it real and I did not want to add stress to my family.

I decided I had to tell my husband and I tried to put on a strong face, but he saw right through it. He prayed over me and claimed that the test would come back just fine. I agreed with him openly, but my heart problems were screeching on the inside. I tried talking to God several times throughout my restless night and all I got was silence. The next morning as I prepared for my appointment, I checked to see if the knot was still there, it was. As I lay on the table watching the monitor show proof of what was going on inside my body, I could not believe my eyes. The radiologist must have taken hundreds of pictures of these round globs that had filled my breasts, they were everywhere. Finally, she told me to sit up so we could talk.

"You're fine, you have several cysts in both breasts, but they are nice and round and I see no signs of cancer." I sat braced for the worst, but I received the most gracious words I had heard in a while. I was fine. Tears welled in my eyes and she left me in the room alone to have my moment. Praise rose from deep down inside of me and all I could do was cry. I called my husband to give him the news and he screamed throughout his job, "Thank You Jesus!" I was so happy that I did not have cancer, but I still had a sad sinking feeling on the inside of me. The story of Jonah kept running through my head and I wanted to talk to God about it, but I was too ashamed at how I had behaved toward Him.

I thought I should not bother Him any that night, after all, He had just brought me out of yet another storm. I was grateful, but I did not want to push my luck with Him. I walked around with this sadness in the pit of my stomach, reading the story of Jonah and trying to see if I was a modern-day runner from Christ. Sunday morning came and I was anxious to hear the word. The pastor seemed to be taking his time this morning, he wanted to talk about his trip and just have a family moment with the congregation. He began to express how he intended on preaching one subject, but as he was on the plane headed home, the Lord told him he had to preach "You can run, but you can't hide" from the book of Jonah. From that moment, I knew without a shadow of a doubt, God called me and He had plans for me.

My heart disease tried to act up and started telling me how wrong I was, but I shut it down instantly. After service ended, I walked into the pastor's office and told him everything. I confessed how I refused God, time and time again. "I wanted to be sure pastor. I didn't want to make a mistake, but now I know, God has called me into the ministry." The pastor anointed me with oil, prayed over me asking God's blessings, and I accepted my call into the ministry.

Your background may be different from mine, but whatever your circumstances, one thing is for sure, you also have a heart condition. As I continued my studies and conversations with the Holy Spirit, I learned I had to give myself a break. I was really beating myself up for refusing God so many times and coming up with so many excuses. But heart issues run deep and they are not easy to break. As a matter of fact, the only way to break these chains is with the help of the Holy Spirit. I was in a spiritual battle for my soul. The Holy Spirit was fighting for me to not trample on the love He had for me by speaking louder than my heart problems over and over again. God the Holy Spirit was helping me to guard my heart. He was telling me I was worth it, my deceived heart was telling me I wasn't. He was telling me I had value, my heart was saying I had nothing to offer. Solomon knew all too well how devastating this battle could be; he had many of his own even though he was a very wise king.

He wrote that we should protect our hearts because the issues of life will flow from it. *Keep thy heart with all diligence; for out of it are the issues of life. (Proverbs 4:23)* The best way to guard our hearts is to ask God to create a clean heart within us as David did in Psalm 51:10. God understands how the heart works and He even knows how to search our hearts; so He is best qualified to create a new one. Notice David did not ask God to clean his heart, he asked God to create a clean heart for him. That is how corrupt and deceitful a heart can get, do not even bother cleaning or repairing it, just throw the whole deceived heart away and start with a fresh clean one; only God can do that. Look at this promise from God telling us He will give us a new heart. *And I will give you a new heart, and I will put a new spirit in you. I will take out your stony, stubborn heart and give you a tender, responsive heart.[b] 27 And I will put my Spirit in you so that you will follow my decrees and be careful to obey my regulations. (Ezekiel 36:26-27 NLT)*

God is happy to remove the old heart of stone,

one that will not let His word pierce through. He will gladly replace it with one that is delighted with His word and responds to His commands. A newly created clean heart is one where the Holy Spirit can dwell. No longer can the issues of past hurts, experiences, traditions, and generational curses cause heart problems for a heart newly created by God. The only issues that spring forth from this new heart of flesh are gratefulness, thankfulness, love, joy, peace, patience, kindness, goodness, faithfulness, gentleness, and self-control. Against such, there is no law.

PRAYER

Most gracious heavenly Father, thank you for creating in me a clean heart and renewing a right spirit within me. For years I lived with a deceived heart and because of that I was defiled. The hurt and pain that I had experienced and bad habits I had learned over the years saturated my heart and found an escape right over my tongue and out of my mouth. Oh what a wretched woman I was, living a life filled with generational curses that had gone unbroken for so many years. I thank you for the promise of giving me a new guarded heart that would allow me to feel your presence and understand your word. Thank you for removing the stony heart from me, one that was hardened against your principles and precepts. My heart has become your dwelling place and it has made me glad. Out of the depths of my heart, I will forever love you and praise you. Amen!

CHAPTER NINE

HE THAT HAS AN EAR

Revelation 3:13 He that hath an ear, let him hear what the Spirit saith unto the churches.

Jesus certainly has a way with words. The simplest phrase from the mouth of our savior can fulfill a hunger in your spirit and plant an appetite for more of His life-giving words. When I first read the words, "He that hath an ear, let him hear," something struck me in the pit of my stomach and I realized there was a greater meaning behind these words. The gospels record Jesus saying this phrase or a form of it 8 times and then another 8 times in the book of Revelation. We all have ears Jesus, so what is the real meaning behind what you are saying? Since we do all have ears, this message is meant for us all; black, white, Asian, Hispanic, Jew, Gentile, male and female – everyone!

I'm sure when Jesus said these words, those who were in His presence, ears perked up. Crowds came to hear Jesus speak, some for different reasons. There were those who came to hear Him hoping He would say something they could use against Him. Others may have come to listen out of curiosity or entertainment hoping to see who would get healed. These remind me of the words of Ezekiel 33:32 NLT *You are very entertaining to them, like someone who sings love songs with a beautiful voice or plays fine music on an instrument. They hear what you say, but they don't act on it!* But there are some who came to hear and apply His life-giving words, allowing them to take root in their hearts. These precious ones not only hear the words of Jesus, but practice them and are strengthened by them.

When Jesus voices this command, "He who has an ear, let him hear," these words bypass the vain listeners and go straight into the heart of the humble changing them from the inside out. *"My soul shall make her boast in the Lord: the humble shall hear thereof, and be glad." (Psalm 34:2)* These humble, willing listeners understand that Jesus is saying something of great importance when He uses this phrase, and they want every drop of it. Not allowing these words to stop at their physical ears, but permitting them to bypass into their own hearing hearts. These true hearers take action and begin the process of getting rid of filth and evil doings in their lives. James, the brother of our Lord, explains it like this: *So get rid of all the filth and evil in your lives, and humbly accept the word God has planted in your hearts, for it has the power to save your souls. But don't just listen to God's word. You must do what it says. Otherwise, you are only fooling yourselves. (James 1:21-22 NLT)* True hearers of God's word are not foolish. Please allow

Jesus to explain the difference between those who hear His words and those who don't:

> *"I will show you what it's like when someone comes to me, listens to my teaching, and then follows it. 48 It is like a person building a house who digs deep and lays the foundation on solid rock. When the floodwaters rise and break against that house, it stands firm because it is well built. 49 But anyone who hears and doesn't obey is like a person who builds a house right on the ground, without a foundation. When the floods sweep down against that house, it will collapse into a heap of ruins." (Luke 6:47-49 NLT)*

Jesus uses an analogy to make sure we not only understand, but we now have a visual of what happens when you let His words go in one ear and out the other. Those who hear, follow a 3-step process.

1. **They Come to Jesus**
2. **They Listen to Jesus**
3. **They Follow Jesus**

Notice, both the hearers and non-hearers built a house, but when the storm came, the non-hearers house collapsed because it had no foundation. The house of the one who followed the 3-step hearing process was able to stand and bear the storm. Just hearing the word of God is not enough to help you stand during times of trials and tribulations, you must obey and be a doer of the word to get those results; you must be an active hearer.

Having an ear to hear what the Spirit is saying, comes with promises. Jesus has something special in store for those who hear His Word and allows it to take root in their hearts.

He that hath an ear, let him hear what the Spirit saith unto the churches; To him that overcometh will I give to eat of the tree of life, which is in the midst of the paradise of God. (Rev 2:7)

He that hath an ear, let him hear what the Spirit saith unto the churches; He that overcometh shall not be hurt of the second death. (Rev 2:11)

He who has an ear, let him hear what the Spirit says to the churches. To the one who is victorious, I will give the hidden manna. I will also give him a white stone inscribed with a new name, known only to the one who receives it. (Revelation 2:17)

I don't know about you, but I want everything Jesus promises. When the Lord spoke to me and told me that I was not able to hear Him because my flesh was louder than His voice, I knew I was dealing with a serious problem. I had a hearing problem. As I began to ponder my life, I knew I had missed out on listening to this glorious voice time and time again. Writing this book is a major step to understand how to hear the Holy Spirit when he speaks to me. Like peeling a banana, I realized that I needed to isolate the voices that were easy for me to hear above the Holy Spirit because they were yelling at me constantly. One by one, I had to dismantle each voice that seemed to drive my actions and decisions when I should have gone a completely different way.

To my surprise, the voices that were shouting at me, were actually hiding in plain sight. These distracting voices had been guiding me for so long that it was difficult for me to recognize just how powerful they were and how harmful they were. I would like to offer some steps in helping to hear God the Holy Spirit's voice, over raging voices:

1. **Repent.** This is always going to be a priority in any spiritual journey. You want to make sure you start off with a clean slate and an open heart to receive what the Spirit says. Removing sinful activities from your life is a must. Refrain from all known sin resisting the devil so that he will flee from you.

2. **Study the Word of God.** The Holy Spirit will never tell you anything that goes against the Word of God. However, if you do not know the Word, you can be easily confused by other voices. Study the Word, meditate on the Word, and hide the Word in your heart so you will not sin against God.

3. **Attend Regular Church Services.** The Bible makes it clear that it is very important for us to hear the word of God through a preacher, one that is sent from Him. Make sure you are under a pastor that teaches directly from the

Word of God and is able to help you understand the scriptures. The Lord will always speak directly to your situation right from the mouth of your shepherd.

4. **Pray.** Staying in communication with the Holy Spirit is critical. Praying is not a one-way communication. It is important to pause and remain quiet with your mind fixed on God to allow Him to respond to you during your prayer communication with Him. Remember, what you are saying to God, is not more important than what He is saying to you.

5. **Avoid Evil Thoughts and Imaginations.** The most common way we miss out on the Holy Spirit's voice, is when He is speaking directly to our heart and mind with a "still soft voice". Because of this, keeping our minds and hearts free of hate, jealousy, lust, and any other evil thoughts will help keep the spiritual ear canal clear for the Holy Spirit's voice only.

6. **Live a Righteous Life.** Live out God's commandments to your best ability. Love God with all of your heart, mind, soul, and strength. Love your neighbor as you love yourself.

As you go on your journey to actively hearing what the Spirit is saying, I pray you identify and destroy all of the screaming chaotic voices of the flesh and the enemy. Remember the better you know Jesus, the better you will hear His voice.

> *John10:26 But ye believe not, because ye are not of my sheep, as I said unto you. 27 My sheep hear my voice, and I know them, and they follow me: 28 And I give unto them eternal life; and they shall never perish, neither shall any man pluck them out of my hand.*

EPILOGUE

I have learned that in this life, voices are lying in secret places of our hearts screaming forcefully, hoping to drown out the voice of the Holy Spirit. As I journeyed to uncover these voices and quiet their rage, I gathered that there is something more sinister going on. There is an entire plot to cause spiritual deafness within God's people. A scheme by the evil one himself. Causing the voices of our human needs, spiritual dryness, relationships, rejections, abuse of grace, death, and unguarded heart to be amplified over God's still soft voice is the largest evil conspiracy yet. If the devil can block you from hearing God's voice, he has the power to manipulate you and ultimately destroy you. You will no longer belong to God, you will belong to him. *"Whoever belongs to God hears what God says. The reason you do not hear is that you do not belong to God." (John 8:47NIV)*

The enemy is hoping to separate us from God and stop us from inheriting eternal life by disabling our hearing.

*"Very truly I tell you, whoever **hears** my word and believes him who sent me has eternal life and will not be judged but has crossed over from death to life." (John 5:24NIV)*

It is time to sharpen our spiritual ear. We cannot afford to allow deafening voices to distract us from the voice of the Holy Spirit. Before that last trumpet sounds, our time would be well spent removing dulling voices and fleshly influences from our heart's mind. We can no longer claim ignorance to God's voice. Our Lord is coming back, when we least expect it. *Remember, therefore, what you have received and **heard**; hold it fast, and repent. But if you do not wake up, I will come like a thief, and you will not know at what time I will come to you. (Revelation 3:3NIV)*

*"Here I am! I stand at the door and knock. If anyone **hears** my voice and opens the door, I will come in and eat with that person, and they with me. To the one who is victorious, I will give the right to sit with me on my throne, just as I was victorious and sat down with my Father on his throne. Whoever has ears, let them hear what the Spirit says to the churches." (Revelation 3:20NIV)*

NOTES

Unless otherwise indicated, all Scripture quotations are from the King James Version (KJV)

Bible, King James Version (KJV)
Bible, New Living Translation (NLT)
Bible, New International Version (NIV)

(1) James Merritt, 52 WEEKS WITH JESUS: Fall in Love with the One Who Changed Everything (Eugene, OR: Harvest House Publishers, 2014), 50.

(2) Dr. David Jeremiah, CAPTURED BY GRACE: No one is Beyond the Reach of a Loving God (Nashville, TN: Thomas Nelson, Inc., 2006), 84.

Dr. David Jeremiah, ESCAPE THE COMING NIGHT (Wheaton, IL: Tyndale House Publishers, 2001), 123.

(3) "Grace." Meriam-Webster.com. 2018. https://www.merriam-webster.com (27 Jun 2018)

(4) "Reject." Meriam-Webster.com. 2018. https://www.merriam-webster.com (27 Jun 2018)

ACKNOWLEDGMENTS

To the only wise God, my Father, the Sovereign Triune God who is the essence of my being, it is because of you that I made it through so many trials and tribulations. You never left me, and for that I thank you from the depths of my soul.

Mr. Dewayne Harris Sr. I cherish the way you look at me. You have always seen the light inside of me, even when I could not. I love you forever.

Mama, Susie Mae Lock, you continue to inspire me. I am keeping your legacy of writing going; your gift will never fade away. Thank you for loving me through so many hard times. You are in my heart forever.

James, Shakara, Nigel, Ahjullah, Dewayne (DJ) and Kamisha, you have seen me go from worse to better and you still call me Mom. What precious gifts God has given me with each of you. I will always come to your rescue.

Terri Suzette Murrell, my baby sister, you have been my inspiration since the day you were born. Thank you for allowing me to shield you from as many bad things as I could. I'm so proud of the loving wife and incredible mother you are. Lawson, Auston, Quinton, and Storri are a reflection of your beautiful heart. I will always cherish you – my first baby doll.

Estella Harris (Ma Dear), you told me you couldn't replace my mother, but you would always be there for me. Thank you for keeping your word. I love you.

Daddy, I realize now that you could only give me what was in your heart. I appreciate you for your part in bringing me into this world. I'm thankful that we reconciled and you accepted Christ as your personal Savior. I love you.

Pastor Marlon Lock and Author Kimberly Lock, thank you for believing in me and always pouring into me. I thank God for the amazing leaders that you are.

My beautiful Lock Family and descendants of Ira and Ossie Lock, you all taught me what family means. We grew up like sisters and brothers and I am so thankful for that. Ida Bell and Shirley Ann Lock, thank you for holding me up when I needed you the most.

KRL Publishing, thank you for helping me make this dream come true. Your professionalism and pursuit of quality have pushed me to heights I was unaware of. Kimberly Rochelle Lock you are a fine gem.

Authors on Fire, you ladies rock. Thank you for

pushing me to get this book done. All of the hours we spent sitting in coffee houses and on the phone has created a bond between us that we will share forever. Sheila, Valecia, Bridgette and Sally I love you.

Dr. Vanessa Renea Liederbach, thank you for writing such a phenomenal Foreword for this book. It seems like you, Pat, Monica, Shelita, Tracy, Marcellus and I have been through it all. I could not wish for a better group of friends. I love you all.

My Unity Gospel House of Prayer family, I am truly honored to serve our Lord and Savior with you all. I love you and let's keep winning souls for Christ.

ABOUT THE AUTHOR

Kara Lock-Harris was born in Philadelphia, Pennsylvania on November 21, 1970; raised from a toddler in Milwaukee, Wisconsin. Kara was the product of a very unlikely and unmarried couple; a young Black girl from Malvern, Arkansas and a White man from Hagerstown, Maryland. Childhood for Kara was no easy feat, as she learned many hard life lessons. Even though rejected by her father, her mother was able to muster up enough love to carry her through. One of her favorite memories of her mom, is when she would read Robert Frost, Edgar Allen Poe and Little House on the Prairie books to her at night. She read so dramatically that Kara was able to imagine the words in her head. Kara fell in love with reading because of her mother's ability to bring a book alive. Kara started writing her own poems and short stories; always dreaming of having her own words in print one day.

Kara, in her younger years, was not always well versed in Scripture, but that did not stop her Savior from covering her and assisting her with His loving Grace. After pain of rejection and many disappointments, Kara later realized that God was always there with her, wanting what was best for her. He often spoke to her during the darkest times of her life, but other voices wouldn't allow her to hear Him. Once she was able to see how the enemy had plugged her spiritual ears, the urge to write how she overcame this deafness in book form was pressing; she needed to share her story to help someone else.

Kara is openly Christian and professes the name of her Lord and Savior Jesus Christ. Kara has attended church since she was a young girl and is currently a member of Unity Gospel House of Prayer in Milwaukee, WI under the leadership of Pastors Marlon and Kimberly Lock. Kara is happily married to Deacon Dewayne Harris and enjoys being a mother and grandmother. She enjoys serving and leading in ministry and it has brought her back to her childhood love – writing. That dream that she had as a young girl to write, God never forgot and He made way for it to come to fruition. Kara owes God her life and the world her story of how He brought a poor young girl back full circle from manifold trials and right into His loving arms.

www.ingramcontent.com/pod-product-compliance
Lightning Source LLC
Chambersburg PA
CBHW052146110526
44591CB00012B/1879